"*Advancing Data Science Education in K-12* offers a unique perspective on data science education from a scholar who has both witnessed and led the development of this emerging discipline. Its breadth and rigor are complemented by Victor Lee's personal stories and observations. It promises to be a definitive text for years to come for researchers and others interested in data science education."

—Joshua Rosenberg, Associate Professor of STEM Education at the University of Tennessee, Knoxville, USA, and co-author of *Data Science in Education Using R*

"This work provides a truly unique perspective, combining Lee's deeply informed experience as a researcher with his incisive acumen for observing and distilling sociopolitical trends in education. Drawing upon both in equal measure, Lee paints an expansive view of the landscape and history of data science education, then culminates the work with a series of provocative punchlines that reveal important new strands of inquiry and illuminate the future of this rapidly growing field. Highly accessible yet packed with nuggets of wisdom, *Advancing Data Science Education in K-12* stands out as that most rare of resources: an essential, go-to primer for those new to the field, and a well of fresh insights and inspiring calls to action for data science educators and researchers, both veteran and new alike."

—Chad Dorsey, President and CEO of The Concord Consortium

"It is a time of rapid curricular change as educators and policymakers grapple with how to deal with a data-rich and AI-mediated future. *Advancing Data Science Education in K-12* is an accessible yet extensive introduction to what researchers know—and, equally important, what we don't yet know—about what it means for youth to think and learn with data. The book is rich in examples of the many ways data science has been taken up in classrooms and other educational spaces. It points to exciting open questions that will require deep collaboration between educators, researchers, and domain experts to address. Perhaps most importantly, it proposes new language that can lend traction and specificity to ongoing conversations and debates in the field. I recommend this book for anyone looking to deepen their understanding of current issues and questions around Data Literacy and Data Science Education."

—Michelle Hoda Wilkerson, Associate Professor in the Berk̲ of Education at University of California–Berkeley, U̲ ̲ ̲ ̲ ̲ ̲ ̲ ̲ ̲ ̲ *Science*

"In this tour-de-force, Victor Lee demonstrates substantial intellectual courage by taking on the field of data science education while it is in a constant state of change. He begins *Advancing Data Science Education in K-12* by questioning whether 'data' is singular or plural and quickly convinces the reader that such attention to detail about words can yield important insights. His discussion of the distinction between 'data literacy' and 'data science' is particularly illuminating, as he offers multiple perspectives that reveal important subtleties not often made clear in print. Throughout, Lee's style is accessible and slyly humorous, guiding the reader through both high-level conceptual discussions and specific examples with equal ease. From readers who are just beginning to learn about data science education to those with substantial knowledge who want a fresh perspective, this is a valuable read."

—Andee Rubin, Principal Scientist at TERC

"The exploding growth in data, the rise of data science, and the need for a coherent way to teach students how to make sense of the world they will inhabit are the core motivations for Victor Lee's provocative, informative, and accessible *Advancing Data Science Education in K-12*. We are at a key inflection point in the development of K-12 Data Science Education, with the initial hype about how data will neatly solve long-standing issues replaced by a more realistic sense of how data can be used (or misused). Lee's thoughtful call for a coherent vision for the field will be extremely valuable for educators, researchers, schools, and policymakers, as well as those interested in ways that data science can transform our educational systems."

—Nicholas J. Horton, Beitzel Professor of Technology and Society (Statistics and Data Science) at Amherst College, USA, and previous Editor of the *Journal of Statistics and Data Science Education*

Advancing Data Science Education in K-12

Advancing Data Science Education in K-12 offers a highly accessible, research-based treatment of the foundations of data science education and its increasingly vital role in K-12 instructional content.

As federal education initiatives and developers of technology-enriched curricula attempt to incorporate the study of data science—the generation, capture, and computational analysis of data at large scale—into schooling, a new slate of skills, literacies, and approaches is needed to ensure an informed, effective, and unproblematic deployment for young learners. Friendly to novices and experts alike, this book provides an authoritative synthesis of the most important research and theory behind data science education, its implementation into K-12 curricula, and clarity into the distinctions between data literacy and data science. Learning with and about data hold equal and interdependent importance across these chapters, conveying the variety of issues, situations, and decision-making integral to a well-rounded, critically minded perspective on data science education.

Students and faculty in teaching, leadership, curriculum development, and educational technology programs will come away with essential insights into the breadth of our current and future engagements with data; the real-world opportunities and challenges data holds when taught in conjunction with other subject matter in formal schooling; and the nature of data as a human and societal construct that demands new competencies of today's learners.

Victor R. Lee is Associate Professor in the Graduate School of Education at Stanford University, USA. His previous books are *Reconceptualizing Libraries: Perspectives from the Information and Learning Sciences* and *Learning Technologies* *and the Body: Integration and Implementation in Formal and Informal Learning Environments*. He received his PhD in Learning Sciences from Northwestern University and holds bachelor's degrees in Cognitive Science and Mathematics from the University of California San Diego.

Advancing Data Science Education in K-12

Foundations, Research, and Innovations

VICTOR R. LEE

Designed cover image: © Getty Images/Teera Konakan

First published 2025
by Routledge
605 Third Avenue, New York, NY 10158

and by Routledge
4 Park Square, Milton Park, Abingdon, Oxon, OX14 4RN

Routledge is an imprint of the Taylor & Francis Group, an informa business

© 2025 Victor R. Lee

The right of Victor R. Lee to be identified as author of this work has been asserted in accordance with sections 77 and 78 of the Copyright, Designs and Patents Act 1988.

All rights reserved. No part of this book may be reprinted or reproduced or utilised in any form or by any electronic, mechanical, or other means, now known or hereafter invented, including photocopying and recording, or in any information storage or retrieval system, without permission in writing from the publishers.

Trademark notice: Product or corporate names may be trademarks or registered trademarks, and are used only for identification and explanation without intent to infringe.

ISBN: 9781032470290 (hbk)
ISBN: 9781032472546 (pbk)
ISBN: 9781003385264 (ebk)

DOI: 10.4324/9781003385264

Typeset in Avenir and Dante
by codeMantra

Contents

	Acknowledgments	*viii*
1	Data Everywhere	1
2	Data Literacy, Data Science, and Terms that Trip Us Up	18
3	Humans Thinking about Data	51
4	Teaching Data Science in Schools	78
5	Learning Data Science Outside of Schools	104
6	Expansive Views for Data Science Education	122
7	Onward—A Data Science Education Research Ecosystem	137
	Index	*151*

Acknowledgments

I look forward to writing acknowledgments sections because writing these usually means the book is complete (or near complete). At the same time, acknowledgments can be challenging to write because there are so many ways in which support and help to make a book possible have been provided, and where to draw the boundary becomes unclear. Still, I will try.

My involvement with this topic began early in my faculty career when I was working at Utah State University. Now, I am at a different university. However, there were so many people and circumstances that made this line of work related to teaching and learning about data, which ultimately became a focus on teaching and learning about data science, into a reality. I worked with talented and hardworking students in Utah. Joel Drake was invaluable and invested in the work that came out of what we internally called "the PAD project" (PAD stood for "physical activity data"), and was part of many studies and papers that came from it. He also graciously coordinated many activities, hacked new things together, and would make the longer drives for fieldwork. He also took a tremendous interest in the work we did with adult athletes and was able to prepare what I think was a really nice and novel dissertation study on adult athletes' science knowledge.

Accompanying Joel in the years when the intensity of classroom design research grew rapidly were Ryan Cain and Jeffrey Thayne. Ryan brought his elementary classroom teaching wisdom and willingness to always lend a hand. Ryan ultimately went on to work on other projects with me that were less about students learning data, but he cut his teeth with me on the PAD project, and I am thrilled for his professional success in the years that followed. Jeff is a deep thinker who was also drawn to many other topics but found a great match with our PAD work, enough so that his dissertation extended it to undergraduate statistics education. Jeff was and is still mightily independent and clever, and he has been able to continue to use those traits in many of his endeavors.

Before this line of work became a multi-year-funded commitment for my lab, Mischy DuMont, Jon Thomas, and Justin Wright were terrific assistants who helped make some of the earliest work happen. Seeing their awe at recognizing what we could make possible for kids with data was confirmation that we were doing worthwhile work, even though there were many technical challenges to hash through as we began on this journey. Other Utah students who had been involved include Kylie Williamson and Mary Briggs, who were my first undergraduate research assistants and were very willing to try out some new things.

My professional colleagues in the Department of Instructional Technology and Learning Sciences and the Emma Eccles Jones College of Education and Human Services created conditions for this line of work to take root. Of special note is my department head at the time, Mimi Recker, who ended up being a frequent collaborator on several other projects (not about learning data though!). I appreciate her willingness to weigh in with spot-on comments about drafts or ideas as I got this body of work into motion. John Edwards was kind enough to be a resource on the newer developments in the programming side of data science, at least for what was new in the mid-late 2010s.

Teachers and students in those projects made the work possible, and I cannot name them as part of confidentiality agreements. But I will thank some wonderful teachers including Anitra Jensen and Dorothy Dobson. Principals, teachers, aides, student teachers, and staff at the schools where we did work—thank you. I also give special thanks to Fred Poole, Travis Thurston (and his family), as well as Ilana Dubovi, for the integral contributions they made to some of the work discussed in this book. Thanks also to Gary Wolf for keeping me connected to the Quantified Self world and inviting me to speak there.

Through National Science Foundation Cyberlearning meetings, Michelle Wilkerson, Joe Polman, Tapan Parikh, and I caught the stated need for more work to be done about how the intersection of technology, data, and student learning needed to be explored, and together we convened the Youth, Learning, and Data Science summit. Michelle, as is always appropriate, deserves extra thanks for doing so much of the work on the ground as Berkeley was hosting things. Kathryn Lanouette also helped make essential things happen for the summit, and later joined on a collaboration that has yielded a level of interest I had not anticipated.

After I moved to Stanford University, I had the privilege to work with more amazing students who were invaluable in helping me do more work to further engage with the growing K-12 data science education movement. Victoria Delaney had been a regular collaborator as we looked at how teachers thought about data, and we also analyzed curriculum materials. Danny Pimentel was a great driver of this work by keeping us reading different things, and while the specific paper we had wanted to write never got written, I like to think the time together was well worth it and still provided good returns. Danny also enthusiastically served as a teaching assistant for the teacher education course on data science that became a topic of one study. Tanya LaMar was the other teaching assistant for the course. Their interest in being part of this course was a great encouragement. Students who hung out with the Data Interactions and STEM Teaching and Learning (DISTAL) lab at Stanford undoubtedly heard some dribblings about this book, and their bodies of work and involvement in other projects with me also kept my curious mind going as I seem to be unable to have only one line of research interests.

More recent project collaborators in this line of data work are Sarah Levine, Dora Demszky, Raquel Coelho, Dorna Abdi, Elizabeth Finlayson Harris, Lena Phalen, Deepak Varuvel Dennison, and Nichole Nomura. Undergraduate students who have shared their time with us include Arnav Gupta and Elanna Mak. Cathy James and Sarah Cullum make so much current work possible and have been gracious collaborators for letting there be data in the strangest places. Christine Bywater gets a special acknowledgment for helping things get done, which then gave me a little bit more time to get this book done. I have had students in my various courses at Stanford connected to data science education who provided valuable conversations and let me float ideas with them that were precursors to what appears in this book.

Outside of university collaborators and students, I have been the beneficiary of a gracious community of scholars who have done foundational work on the topic of this book and were willing to talk with me, and find some of my ideas interesting: Andee Rubin, Bill Finzer, Tim Erickson, Rob Gould, Suyen Machado, Cliff Konold, Tony Petrosino, Hollylynne Lee (sorry to complicate both our professional lives with our shared last name), Rich Lehrer, Nick Horton, and Sherry Hsi. Thanks to Shiyan Jiang and Josh Rosenberg for our adventures in journal guest editing that also gave us time to speak to the important opportunities to think about data science education across the curriculum. And, here is where I get nervous because I could probably list names for days of other unnamed colleagues who shared wisdom with me or were a catalyst for some of my thinking. To all who fit this description, thank you.

The Concord Consortium has been a remarkable champion of data science education, and Chad Dorsey's and Kate Miller's combined leadership and ability to get all things done and willingness to include me in their activities is so greatly appreciated. The spaces I get to share with Lynn Stephens, Dan Damelin, and Talya St. Clair from Concord have been very helpful as well. Zarek Drozda, executive director of Data Science 4 Everyone, has genuinely impressed me with his preternatural ability to lead complex initiatives so early in his career and graciously include me in some of them. Thanks to all of these individuals and many more, I am wiser and connected to data science education world—and hope to stay connected.

Michelle Wilkerson, named above, but a tremendous and generous thought partner, gets additional mention as a co-conspirator and presence. People who know Michelle know she is both amazing and modest, and it is always a pleasure for me to work with her. So as I teased, Michelle, you get acknowledged twice.

Several projects named above and in the book were funded by the National Science Foundation, through grant numbers 1054280, 1645559, and 2241483. The opinions expressed in this book are my own and do not necessarily reflect those of the National Science Foundation. I am also grateful to the National Academies of Science, Engineering, and Medicine (NASEM) and in particular Heidi Schweingruber and Amy Stephens for allowing me to be in spaces where important ideas about data science education are synthesized. I do want to disclose that as I wrote this book, I was serving on multiple NASEM committees producing reports but made a very intentional point to have those activities and any writing I do for that work and this book be completely separated. Some topics I might have discussed here, I refrained from addressing so as to keep things separate between those commitments. Heidi and Amy, as well as Nick Horton, spurred my appreciation for the messy challenge about constantly changing topics that I discuss in the final chapter of the book.

This book was being written when ChatGPT came out and, because of that, my professional life got very hectic. In case anyone is wondering, all of the text in this book has been written by me, the human. The only AI that was involved in writing was Grammarly, which, in the version I used, could only help me catch typos and flag some sentences that were too hard for even me to understand even though I wrote them. The copyediting team and multiple additional reads by me and some trusted colleagues still caught things the AI did not. In the final push to get this book done, which kept getting delayed because of all the AI in education activities that rapidly filled my calendar, I benefited from the patience and assistance of many people who could tend to things when I went dark on communications. There are too many to be able to name.

I give a special thanks to my editor at Routledge, Daniel Schwartz, who championed the book and was incredibly understanding about delays on my side and willing to give me the extensions I needed due to generative AI in education activities and unexpected things popping up frequently that required my attention.

Finally, Jalila, Cailin, and Vivian have my unending love and gratitude for being them and for being with me.

Data Everywhere 1

Data is everywhere. Or is it that data *are* everywhere? Grammatically, the word "data" is itself the plural form of "datum", in a similar way that "media" is the plural form of the word "medium". However, it is pretty rare to have a conversation where someone outright uses the word "datum", and it has now gotten to the point that referring to data as singular has become normalized. For instance, the *New York Times* style guide (Siegel & Connolly, 2015) allows for use of the word data as a singular or plural. Therefore, data is and data are. However, the seventh edition style manual for the American Psychological Association (APA) (2019), currently the most recent edition, is very explicit that datum is singular and data are plural. Verb usage should conform to that in writing. We look to two potential models for how to proceed in our use of the word "data" and immediately find contradictory guidance.

In a book that is about K-12 data science education, why open with consideration about the proper grammatical usage of the word data (or datum)? The reason for this is that it is in many ways reflective of our current state of affairs in this new data science education field. Data science education is something that is being actively discussed, whether by policymakers, educators, researchers, funders, universities, or employers. It may have some unknown original sourcing and expectations when the term had been initially used for what it meant.[1] However, similar to the word "data", its increased uptake and continued embedding into many different social spheres over time has enabled a shift in usage and reference. When it comes to K-12 education, it is becoming less clear to many what we are talking about with data science

DOI: 10.4324/9781003385264-1

education for primary and secondary levels and what, if any, is the body of core knowledge to inform its development and growth as an area for educational innovation. This is, of course, assuming that we are even interested in advancing data science education in K-12—which may not be a point of agreement (see commentaries and arguments about the matter from Jo Boaler, Brian Conrad, Ben Ford, Rafe Mazzeo, and Jelani Nelson in Boaler et al., 2024). It has stirred some controversy, such as in the development and eventual approval of the 2023 California Mathematics Framework—a guideline document regarding K-12 mathematics instruction that acknowledged the increasing importance of data in our lives. That controversy has led to a procedural whiplash where just a few years ago, high school "data science" courses were deemed as allowable for fulfilling high school mathematics course requirements but then following a decision in 2024, the same courses were deemed insufficient and would no longer count toward fulfilling those same mathematics course requirements that they had fulfilled previously. In some respects, this has become another front in the longstanding "math wars" (see Wilson, 2003, for a summary of the earlier math wars) where what counts as mathematics and what should be taught as mathematics stirs passions from multiple sides.

But let us assume that regardless of these disagreements about mathematics curriculum and pathways, we *do* want to advance data science education in K-12. Let us also assume we do not feel bound to this being strictly the concern of mathematics educators and math education advocates, although there are certainly relevant overlaps. Various activities are afoot whether it is the formation of advocacy groups, expert convenings, position statements by politicians, and policy documents to bring data science education into primary and secondary schools. Given what feels like a rising educational interest, we should consider: What do we already know from the research literature that is of relevance to these efforts? What projects relevant to data science education have been pursued and are worth emulating (or avoiding)? What gaps do we have that remain fruitful for future research? What kind of future might we pursue for this thing we are starting to call K-12 data science education?

Such are questions that have a research bent, owing largely to this book being written by an academic researcher. However, while this book is heavy on what the research says, the grand hope is that there are still nuggets for others who are interested in data science education, regardless of their roles in the education system. The primary focus, however, will not be on how to enact specific classroom lessons, providing assessment rubrics, or policy guidelines. Also, this is not a book that aims to be the resource that teaches someone to become a data scientist (see Estrellado et al., 2020, for something like that). What it does attempt to do is help people who want a place to start so that they can devise their own projects and questions to inform the larger endeavor of advancing data science education in K-12. A long time ago, I began my own journey into this space and had to do a lot of reading and talking with people to learn what I know now. This book is a distillation of that journey—one that I consider to be ongoing—with the hope of making it easier for others to participate in this growing field.

The contents of this book, while reporting and relying heavily on existing peer-reviewed research, is colored by my own perspective. That perspective takes seriously that many questions within the purview of data science education overlap substantially with work that has been done previously and continues to be done in statistics education. At the same time, enough has changed in the past few decades that it does seem sensible to pursue data science education and not consider it simply a rebranding of statistics education. It also is not simply computer science education or math education. Those changes include who is participating and influential in these spheres, whether through popular opinion or academic regard, what techniques and technologies are readily available, and increasing public awareness of some longstanding challenges that have existed in society, such as who is included and who is excluded as data science and concomitantly, data science education, progresses.

Why Is Everyone So Interested in Data Lately?

Data is (or are?) hot right now. Availability and abundance are two key reasons for renewed interest in data. Data have long been collected for a range of human activities, whether scientific inquiry that involved conducting experiments and recording data or for strategic decision-making. A fascinating historical account is provided in *How Data Happened* (2023) by Chris Wiggins and Matthew Jones, which traces the development of statistics and key figures such as Quetelet, Pearson, Nightingale, Fisher, and Tukey. Yet the rise of and increased societal reliance on the internet has made data quicker to generate and store. Computational power has increased, computing devices have shrunk in size but multiplied in number, and storage capabilities have grown. Various sensationalized calculations of how much data are produced in a given day have been offered, with one number often circulated being 2.5 quintillion bytes (2.5 × 10^{18} or 2.5 billion billions) a day (e.g., Roque & Ram, 2019). This is the "big" of big data, which is also characterized by the "3 Vs" of velocity, volume, and variety. Some have likened data to "the new oil" (which is used to imply the sheer abundance and massive profit opportunities but can also be extended as a metaphor to foreground problems like leaks and pollution—see Hirsch (2014)).

Thanks to so much data, science and industry have advanced. However, the services and experiences we encounter, especially with information, have changed in dramatic ways. We can now get customized recommendations for products, services, and social connections; generate insight through analytics about what variables are influencing what group of people under what circumstances; and make better predictions whether they are used for the stock market, the weather, or sports. From a hyper-rationalist point of view, more data also ought to be the basis of better decision-making (more on that to come later). With data being able to do all of this, it seems people ought to be empowered to use data in potent ways.

But those are the optimistic and idealistic takes. Data can also obfuscate, be overly reductive, and may be held in too high a esteem as a tool for knowing and being in the world. It can be downright offensive to reduce some of our most treasured aspects of human experience to individual measurements and labels. Treating messy social issues as quantitative optimization problems, which work with data tends to do, can end up causing more harm than good. This approach can also unevenly distribute harms and benefits. For example, if we have a web service and want to maximize the amount of time users spend watching video on our website of video content, we may gain some good by having an engrossed and receptive audience. However, we could also be causing serious harm in that it is not in the best interest of people or society to have everyone spend all their time watching videos residing on one specific website. There may also be unintended risks such as amplifying misinformation or problematic content. For instance, this is a concern that has been raised recently in the context of affecting young peoples' mental health (Haidt, 2024).

These more critical and skeptical perspectives suggest that we should focus our data science education energies not just on helping people to harness data's power but rather on understanding risks and equipping people to draw the line on what will and will not be tolerated in a world where data are everywhere. Similar to campaigns to reduce unwanted pregnancies or illegal drug use, including this critical view of data can serve as cautionary, preventative, and safety-oriented for the betterment of individuals and society. The current regimes of data collection, analysis, and usage may be alarming and concerning and something that requires focused educational efforts. Stated simply, we may need to teach about data to improve societal outcomes.

Ultimately, much of our world runs on data, and people are both producing and affected by those data. That shows no signs of abating, even though new regulations may affect how data are used. Given this is already and will continue to be part of our lives, and the lives of students in the future, we do need to teach about it.

Data, Jobs, and a Small Illustration

Because data are permeating so many parts of our lives, the current sense is that it will be an important part of our future economy. McKinsey Global Institute (2016) estimates many trillions of dollars and substantial productivity increases in the economy to be tied to or affected by more use of data in the workplace, with the exact amounts varying across sectors. Universities and students are responding to this. Data science undergraduate majors awarded increased by 968% from 2020 to 2022, according to data compiled by the National Center for Education Statistics (Pierson, 2023). This all sounds like data science has the potential to be important for future job opportunities, assuming there will be jobs needing those backgrounds.

Indeed, evidence suggests that job growth is looking good for data science. In the United States, the Bureau of Labor Statistics (2024) forecasts the job outlook to have 35% growth from 2022 to 2032, much faster than average. This is their third highest growth rate, behind only wind turbine service technicians and nurse practitioners. Wind turbine service technicians and nurse practitioners? Certainly, both occupations represent important and valuable work, but that may seem unexpected as we don't hear about those in the news or business reports to nearly the same degree. But I include and will expound on that because to pause and consider how to make sense of this is illustrative of some of the foundational thinking that will be needed for data scientists.

6 Advancing Data Science Education in K-12

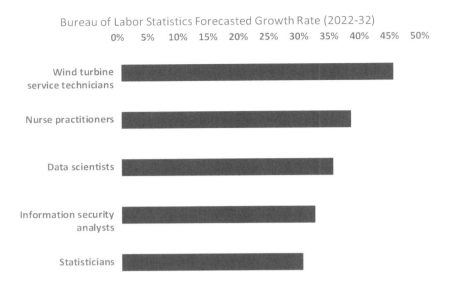

Figure 1.1 Forecasted growth of occupations according to the US Bureau of Labor Statistics (BLS). The five occupations with the highest growth rates are shown.

First, percentage growth is a specific kind of quantity. If there were 1,000 data scientists in the world and 100 wind turbine service technicians, and each were going to add 100 jobs, then that percentage growth measure might feel misleading (10% for data scientists, 100% for wind turbine service technicians). This means we need to take into account how those numbers are calculated before we infer that there are more jobs to be had in one area or another, because that is a different statement than higher growth rate. It turns out that Bureau of Labor Statistics (BLS) has reported 11,200 wind turbine technician jobs in 2022 whereas there were 168,900 data scientist jobs in the same time period—so the point holds. In the next ten years, assuming this is a simple ratio calculation, we can predict about 59,000 new data scientist jobs and about 5,000 wind turbine technician jobs. So BLS's estimates have wind turbine technician jobs growing at a rate of 45%, which is indeed larger than the data scientist rate of 35%.

How about nurse practitioners? In 2022, there were 323,900 nurse practitioners, and the forecasted 2022–2032 growth was 38%. That would mean around 123,000 new nurse practitioner jobs. This is a larger number than either wind turbine technicians or data scientists. Maybe we should really be putting our primary focus on medical training and nursing in K-12!

Also, we should consider that these are estimates, both for the 2022 numbers and for the forecasted ones. Do we know that there were exactly 168,900 data scientist jobs? There were no layoffs nor promotions to management that make that number a little uncertain? Did the BLS go door to door and count everyone's job by hand? If they relied on tax records, did they group "data analyst" and "data scientist" together or treat those as different? What about "Data Scientist II" versus "Data Scientist I"?, a distinction that human resources may create to differentiate required training and pay scale. If one goes further down Figure 1.1, the job of Statistician appears. In the counting, was there careful differentiation between data scientists and statisticians? Let's assume for now they are distinct. However, this points to a larger challenge. There are likely people in the workplace who will be doing work with data who are not branded as data scientists (or statisticians)—whether it has to do with budgets, inventory, marketing contacts, human resources, or whatnot. One might object that those individuals are not doing "data science", because they are not using advanced computational algorithms and machine learning techniques. But if we consider the 168,900 data scientists in the BLS database, can we be certain that everyone who is in the job of data scientist is working with computational algorithms and machine learning? Many may be spending most of their time cleaning data, which is informally the largest time commitment for people working in data science.

I will concede that despite this digression to the messiness of data, there are a lot of signs suggesting that data science will have an important role for employment and the economy. However, a larger point is that to know data in powerful ways so that it can be used in the context of work (and other contexts as well), there are decisions made that make the data look the ways that they do. And beneath the numbers are more complicated situations. While it seems the future economy and future work will be using data a lot, I would argue it is best to be able to work with data in ways that are wise and able to take into consideration questions like the ones posed in this example, which can be easy to overlook or disregard. This holds true whether or not someone formally becomes a data scientist (or statistician, or nurse practitioner, or just about any other job that might require interfacing with data).

Data and a New Era of Artificial Intelligence (AI)

At the time that this book was being prepared, we also had a tremendous explosion of interest in AI thanks in part to the release of ChatGPT in late 2022 and worldwide fascination with generative AI. ChatGPT is a chatbot technology that produced remarkably good written responses to written prompts. Where we previously had clunky chatbots on websites that were not very good at answering our basic product and service questions, we suddenly had chatbot technology that would be able to write about any topic in whatever styles we requested. We could, in a matter of seconds, have a full screenplay, essay, short story, sample legal document, or speech generated by typing that request. That was just for text. Generative AI was also enabling dynamic image, sound, and movie generation. Organizations like Khan Academy rushed to develop sophisticated and dynamic tutors for schools. A lot of hand-wringing ensued about what this would mean for the world as we had known it before. Schools were immediately worried that students would use this technology to cheat and stop doing their own assigned work (the early evidence on this has suggested that was not the immediate reaction in K-12, see Lee et al., 2024). Actors and writers went on strike and included new restrictions on AI as part of their agreements (Scherer, 2023, 2024). Lawsuits about copyright infringement (Samuelson, 2023) and cautionary tales of professionals caught using generative AI when they probably should not have made the news, due to generative AI's propensity to generate inaccurate information.

Still, the buzz around AI, most recently envisioned as the generative type (rather than classic symbolic AI or another variety), is there. However, AI has been around for quite some time,[2] and in many instances—including those using generative AI—has been enabled to perform well because of work involving data. From large sets of data, whether scraped from the internet or existing in public repositories, systems have been trained with machine learning to produce behaviors we would have considered as requiring intelligence. Indeed, much of the hype around data science had been the AI possibilities that were emerging as a result of working with large amounts of data. One read that I would recommend for those interested in the development of (and some risks associated with) AI based on data is Artificial Unintelligence (2018) by Meredith Broussard.

It is important to know that not all AI requires data or data science, and not all data or data science is used for AI. However, the connection is strong enough with these frontier uses that even with AI seeming to take more of the educational and workforce spotlight, data science is still there and is a large part of what makes much of that AI. Increasingly, generative AI tools are showing greater ability to work with data on demand by generating some insights and visualizations when given a data set and prompts. However, just as is the case for computer science, the ability for AI to perform well on tasks does not negate the need for people to understand how these work. Computer scientists still need to know computer science even if they have AI tools to write code for them. These tools and features are showing time and again that they require oversight. But this will ultimately be part of the productivity and economic boost that McKinsey Global Institute (2016), mentioned above, had been suggesting was coming.

Will People Need to Learn Data Science Still?

With the capabilities of generative AI to produce a variety of writings on demand, produce images, music, and videos, much anxiety has come about what is left for humans to do. Some of this is expressed as angst about jobs and what jobs will exist. Some of this comes out as fear that time invested in studying something that AI can perform decently—such as quickly writing computer code—will have been for naught as the humans doing the skills will not be necessary.

However, I would argue the way to think about this shift is that for the most part, AI is going to change the way we do work but not eliminate the need for humans to be doing the work. An often used quote to reframe what the future of AI and work will be in the future comes from Stanford Professor of Radiology, Curtis Langlotz: "AI won't replace radiologists, but radiologists who use AI will replace those who don't" (2019). Similarly, we could expect that AI won't replace data scientists, but it is possible that knowing how to use AI well in service of data science is going to be important for future data science work. Also, as stated above, the development and training of AI relies heavily on data science—so we have still more reason to expect a continued need for people to know data science.

Moreover, generative AI currently has a reputation for being a bit weak when it comes to doing mathematics. While some plugins could be used, let's consider chatbots of 2023, such as ChatGPT 4. In Figure 1.2 there is an example from my own interactions with ChatGPT on an arithmetic problem.

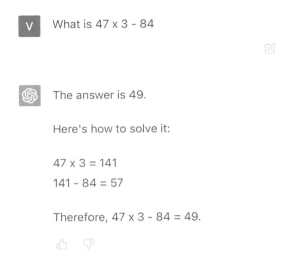

Figure 1.2 A screen capture from an exchange with ChatGPT 4 asking for a mathematical computation.

Following standard order of operations, the answer to this should be 57. In the summary of "Here's how to solve it", the arithmetic steps are correct—47 times 3 is indeed 141 and 141 minus 84 is 57; 57 is the answer. But at the beginning and end of ChatGPT's response, it incorrectly stated the answer was 49.

Stated in simplified terms, the reason for this is that when posed with what we recognize as a mathematics problem, ChatGPT does not switch to calculator mode. Rather, its impressive abilities reside in putting together cohesive seeming sequences of symbols (words, for instance) that are likely to be together given extensive training from data. For whatever reason, there is some way in which this combination of numbers-as-symbols has tended to appear in ways that make 49 likely. But in mathematical computations, we do not (or aspire not to) rely on patterns of probabilistic co-occurrence. Rather, we engage in computation following certain rules we learn about the number system and operations, a different mode of generating responses.

Data science will be more complicated in many respects, and there are a number of capabilities where one can provide a data set and some requests to ChatGPT or another chatbot and have some initial graphs and conclusions derived. But the risk of errors like what is shown above still exists. It is a similar situation to getting information on the internet. There are a lot of results returned on a given search, and, many times, the information can look pretty consistent across sites or just sound right. However, it is still not the same as assuming that the results are indeed "right". In light of misinformation crises and disinformation campaigns, we are recognizing that diligence and careful consideration are necessary are our searches for information online. Similarly, we can expect the same for AI. It may produce things that look right and, on many occasions, return acceptable results. But we need to be vigilant still and be prepared to understand and audit what AI produces as well as know what queries and prompts we should best use at different parts of the data analysis process for a given problem. AI may make some things we do in data science faster or modify some workflows, but humans still need to develop their own knowledge and capabilities with data science.

My Research Journey into Data Science Education

Before going further, I will share a little of my own journey that led to this book. As stated earlier, many years ago I began to do research on how to help students—primarily upper elementary and middle school, although occasionally high schoolers—to do work with data (e.g., Lee & DuMont, 2010; Lee & Thomas, 2011). It was a slight pivot from my earlier work that focused on the kinds of visual representations used to teach science in schools, but that earlier work also directly motivated my journey into thinking about learning with data. It turned out that despite science having a fundamental relationship to visualizations of data (Latour, 1990; Lemke, 1998) it was pretty hard to have substantive engagement with data in the context of a school science class. It took a lot of time, there were a number of things that could go wrong, and not all students were in the same place with their mathematics and statistics knowledge. So thanks to funding from the National Science Foundation, I began thinking more about data—especially data that young people could collect and analyze about themselves.

Research involves a mix of implementing studies, interpreting the outcomes, and reviewing the literature—not necessarily in that order (although sometimes it does). It is very cyclical, and that meant I would be continually reading new things along the way. What was especially important for me was that there had been a good amount of prior research around data work. A lot of this was based in mathematics education, but there was also a separate body of work that was statistics education. This included things like how averages can be misunderstood, what are good ways to sequence data analysis across a curriculum, or what are some tendencies for young people when they try to represent groups of data in some way. Certainly, there was far more, and some of that will appear in Chapters 3–5. I was fortunate to be able to have conversations with generous people who had been doing that earlier work before I got involved, and that helped me learn still more.

As the 2010s were taking off, new approaches to using technology in education were gaining more ground (Borgman, 2008), more researchers were identifying a need to speak more to learning with and about data. This coincided with the growth of data science outside of education, but fields such as learning analytics and educational data mining were coming into their own having followed their own trajectories. With three colleagues, Joseph Polman, Michelle Wilkerson, and Tapan Parikh, we secured funding (from the National Science Foundation) for an academic convening to have more discussions about data, technology, and learning. We convened in Berkeley in 2016, and a number of common interests related to data were expressed. Ultimately, this led to various activities, including a special issue on data science and learning that was edited by Wilkerson and Polman (2020) and a commissioned paper on some of the newer ways in which data were being used in middle and secondary science education by Wilkerson and me (Lee & Wilkerson, 2018). There were already some curriculum efforts for introducing data science into high schools happening, and more people were taking notice.

Ultimately, interest in data and data science as a topic in schools took off. This enticed a number of really motivated and thoughtful people into doing research in the area and boosted some people who had work recently under way. Yet it was becoming apparent that there were many like me who joined this community after coming from other lines of work and were still acquainting themselves with the literature. Many did not know it existed, incorrectly assuming that because data science sounded so new, there must not have been relevant prior work. I considered my own experience getting acquainted with the research literature related to learning with data as a valuable one, although it was certainly time-consuming. I also was learning new lessons in my own work that seemed worth sharing, even for just practical purposes. A number of the generous mentors who helped guide me on the journey were retiring, and I found myself sharing more and more what I had learned throughout the 2010s with others. Ultimately, the decision came to prepare this book—what is intended to be a resource for those getting started or just interested in seeing how this topic has been tackled. The best outcome I can think of, as a researcher, is that this book comes in useful so that future researchers can go and do more interesting work than I could have but can also appreciate what others have taught to me. And, of course, it would definitely be nice for this to ultimately contribute in some way to a positive net impact on efforts to bring data science education into K-12 settings.

The Contents of this Book

This book is organized into seven chapters. While there may be some people who will read this cover to cover—and the book is written with the hope that is what readers will do—I would not doubt that perhaps a section or a chapter will ultimately be shared by itself. Therefore, the writing of sections is intended to keep things modular such that the chapters are not absolutely dependent on what was said in preceding chapters in order to be understood. For those who do like to go from beginning to end, there is a logic to the order. Obviously, this is Chapter 1 and serves to just prepare readers for what is coming next. It acknowledges that to many people, especially education researchers, data science education in K-12 education seems like a big deal. But there are a number of things that are unresolved, in dispute, or arguably important to be sure to consider. It acknowledges that there is work done in the past and more recently that could be useful as a research community develops to think through both old and new questions about how to teach about data in schools.

Chapter 2 bares some uncertainties we have when saying we want to promote data science education in K-12. There are debates as to what data science is, whether it is different from other things that we already try to encourage, and what we are hoping to teach under this umbrella of K-12 data science. While it may not ultimately resolve disagreements, the goal is to give some ways to talk about what is the nature of disagreements. I put forward some of the different ways we are tending to think about K-12 data science and how it seems to sit relative to mentions of "data literacy", share different ways of viewing what is at the core of data science, and situate the view of data science and data science education adopted in this book.

In Chapter 3, the emphasis is on how people think and learn about data. Some classic cognitive psychology work related to statistical reasoning is discussed. Work from developmental psychology is presented as well. This chapter also covers some of the insights about viewing data that statistics educators have identified. Continuing with the contribution of statistics education research, key ideas related to data and important properties of data are discussed. Topics range from judgment under uncertainty to visualization comprehension to distribution being an important, although underemphasized, idea for students to learn.

Chapter 4 focuses on the ways in which K-12 data science education has been introduced in schools. Mathematics instruction has been one long-standing context, and data-related content is part of mathematics standards across grade levels. However, there are also forms of explicitly standalone curricula—whereby a course is created for the purpose of teaching data science as an explicit subject of its own. A complementary approach has also emerged and been advocated recently (Jiang et al., 2022) that is to have data science integrated across the curriculum. This integrative approach situates data science education within other subject areas—such as teaching data science with social studies. Examples from recent projects spanning from Art to Language Arts are shared here. The work of supporting teachers in learning to teach data science in its K-12 form is also discussed.

While the focus of this book is on K-12 data science education, implying that the goal is to focus on what happens in the schoolhouse, Chapter 5 discusses research that comes from out-of-school settings. It is my view that there are interesting insights and additional perspectives that can come from looking at settings other than schools, even if one ultimately wants to circle back to the teaching and learning that happens in schools (Lee, 2015). This is because the different constraints and circumstances in other settings help to make visible what is possible. There is also value in seeing what helps make certain activities or practices work and meaningful in the non-school settings where they reside. Also, it allows for some consideration of how students might use these ideas outside of the classroom. Topics covered here include data science in sports, at home, and in digital media (including social media).

Throughout the book, there are references to ways of thinking about data science that go beyond knowing certain statistical ideas, technical processes, and algorithms. Chapter 6 is an explicit call out of these approaches—some of which are critical (in a "critical theory" sense) in that they address issues of power and injustice—and others that are thinking more broadly about data and what we consider to be under the umbrella label of "data". Recognizing that each could merit their own book and have importance along, for the sake of providing a starting overview for newcomers, I refer to these collectively as "expansive views". In this chapter, I summarize some features of expansive views and describe some new ideas and constructs that are based in these views that have already been named in the literature.

Finally, in Chapter 7, I reflect on the larger systems in which data science education and specifically data science education *research* reside. While explicitly not a statement on nor guidance for formal policies, as those require a different body of expertise, this chapter does argue for the importance of continued work and research in data science education, including the work of keeping it visible and advocating for it publicly. Also, this book is not going to cover all the things that are pertinent, especially as new reports and books come out. Some other valuable books that are syntheses are summarized and recommended here.

Notes

1 A brief historical account is provided in Mike et al. (2023) tracing the term "data science education" to a workshop supported by the National Science Foundation and the Association for Computing Machinery in 2015 to address job needs.
2 For a summary of the long history of AI and education, see Doroudi (2023).

References

American Psychological Association. (2019). *Publication Manual of the American Psychological Association*, 7th Edition. Washington, DC: American Psychological Association

Boaler, J., Conrad, B., Ford, B., Mazzeo, R., & Nelson, J. (2024). Three views on the California Math Framework. *Notices of the American Mathematical Society, 71*(6), 797–805. https://doi.org/10.1090/noti2957

Borgman, C. L., Abelson, H., Dirks, L., Johnson, R., Koedinger, K. R., Linn, M. C., ... Szalay, A. (2008). *Fostering learning in the networked world: The cyberlearning opportunity and challenge*. Retrieved from https://www.nsf.gov/pubs/2008/nsf08204/nsf08204.pdf

Broussard, M. (2018). *Artificial unintelligence: How computers misunderstand the world*. Cambridge: MIT Press.

Bureau of Labor Statistics, U.S. Department of Labor. (2024). *Occupational Outlook Handbook, Data Scientists*. Retrieved from https://www.bls.gov/ooh/math/data-scientists.htm (visited August 3, 2024).

Doroudi, S. (2023). The intertwined histories of artificial intelligence and education. *International Journal of Artificial Intelligence in Education, 33*(4), 885–928. https://doi.org/10.1007/s40593-022-00313-2

Estrellado, R. A., Freer, E., Rosenberg, J. M., & Velásquez, I. C. (2020). *Data science in education using R*. London: Routledge.

Haidt, J. (2024). *The anxious generation: How the great rewiring of childhood is causing an epidemic of mental illness*. New York: Random House.

Hirsch, D. D. (2014). The glass house effect: Big data, the new oil, and the power of analogy. *Maine Law Review, 66*(2), 373.

Jiang, S., Lee, V. R., & Rosenberg, J. M. (2022). Data science education across the disciplines: Underexamined opportunities for K-12 innovation. *British Journal of Educational Technology, 53*(2), 1073–1079. https://doi.org/10.1111/bjet.13258

Latour, B. (1990). Drawing things together. In M. Lynch & S. Woolgar (Eds.), *Representation in scientific practice* (pp. 19–68). Cambridge: MIT Press.

Lee, V. R. (2015). Looking at how technology is used with the bodies over there to figure out what could be done with the technology and bodies right here. In V. R. Lee (Ed.), *Learning technologies and the body: Integration and implementation in formal and informal learning environments* (pp. 167–184). New York, NY: Routledge.

Lee, V. R., & DuMont, M. (2010). An exploration into how physical activity data-recording devices could be used in computer-supported data investigations. *International Journal of Computers for Mathematical Learning, 15*(3), 167–189. https://doi.org/10.1007/s10758-010-9172-8

Lee, V. R., Pope, D., Miles, S., & Zárate, R. C. (2024). Cheating in the age of generative AI: A high school survey study of cheating behaviors before and after the release of ChatGPT. *Computers and Education: Artificial Intelligence, 7*, 100253. https://doi.org/10.1016/j.caeai.2024.100253

Lee, V. R., & Thomas, J. M. (2011). Integrating physical activity data technologies into elementary school classrooms. *Educational Technology Research and Development, 59*(6), 865–884. https://doi.org/10.1007/s11423-011-9210-9

Lee, V. R., & Wilkerson, M. (2018). *Data use by middle and secondary students in the digital age: A status report and future prospects*. Commissioned Paper for the National Academies of Sciences, Engineering, and Medicine, Board on Science Education, Committee on Science Investigations and Engineering Design for Grades 6–12. Washington, DC.

Lemke, J. L. (1998). Multiplying meaning: Visual and verbal semiotics in scientific text. In J. Martin & R. Veel (Eds.), *Reading science*. New York: Routledge.

McKinsey Global Institute. (2016). *The age of analytics: Competing in a data-driven world*. Retrieved from https://www.mckinsey.com/capabilities/quantumblack/our-insights/the-age-of-analytics-competing-in-a-data-driven-world

Mike, K., Kimelfeld, B., & Hazzan, O. (2023). The birth of a new discipline: Data science education. *Harvard Data Science Review, 5*(4). https://doi.org/10.1162/99608f92.280afe66

Pierson, S. (2023). Data analytics, data science degrees see large increases. *Amstat News*, (538), 16–21.

Roque, N. A., & Ram, N. (2019). tsfeaturex: An R package for automating time series feature extraction. *Journal of Open Source Software, 4*(37). https://doi.org/10.21105/joss.01279

Samuelson, P. (2023). Generative AI meets copyright. *Science, 381*(6654), 158–161. https://doi.org/10.1126/science.adi0656

Scherer, M. (2023). *New WGA labor agreement gives Hollywood writers important protections in the Era of AI*. Retrieved from https://cdt.org/insights/new-wga-labor-agreement-gives-hollywood-writers-important-protections-in-the-era-of-ai/

Scherer, M. (2024). *The SAG-AFTRA strike is Over, but the AI fight in Hollywood is just beginning*. Retrieved from https://cdt.org/insights/the-sag-aftra-strike-is-over-but-the-ai-fight-in-hollywood-is-just-beginning/

Siegel, A. M., & Connolly, W. (2015). *The New York Times manual of style and usage: The official style guide used by the writers and editors of the world's most authoritative newspaper*. New York: Crown.

Wiggins, C., & Jones, M. L. (2023). *How data happened: A history from the age of reason to the age of algorithms*. New York: WW Norton & Company.

Wilkerson, M. H., & Polman, J. L. (2020). Situating data science: Exploring how relationships to data shape learning. *Journal of the Learning Sciences, 29*(1), 1–10. https://doi.org/10.1080/10508406.2019.1705664

Wilson, S. M. (2003). *California dreaming: Reforming mathematics education*. New Haven, CT: Yale University Press.

Data Literacy, Data Science, and Terms that Trip Us Up

2

When we talk about data science, what exactly is it we are talking about? In Chapter 1, I discussed the growth in data and in jobs that are called "data scientist" that contribute to the interest in K-12 data science education. Perhaps frustratingly for some readers, the term "data science" was not defined there. That was because I wanted to take more space to delve a little bit further into what different people are saying it means and how that has led to complicated takes on whether something is or is not data science, whether something is "just" data literacy, and if there is actually something new there or we have invented an empty term. Also, while I do want to acknowledge that as broadly represented, professional data science seems to have some sophisticated tools and technical terms that are used (e.g., cosine similarity, a way of determining how similar two vectors are to one another). I will include some of those here, but, aside from the most recent example, refrain from defining them. I trust that anyone interested in those can turn to other sources like guidebooks or trustworthy websites to learn what specific terms mean, because this book is not meant to be a technical guide to data science. However, in several places, this chapter will at least mention some of those technical terms because this chapter is where I talk more about how some people characterize data science (i.e., as a highly technical and advanced field and requiring mastery of ideas like cosine similarity) and the associated implications for data science education in K-12 (e.g., we must teach cosine similarity). With that said, it is fine for readers to see unfamiliar technical terms and know that they refer to something specialized in more advanced, typically postsecondary-level data science work but readers are not accountable for understanding them in order to get something from this chapter.

DOI: 10.4324/9781003385264-2

Anyway, defining data science can be a fool's errand. While it might be nice to have a checklist that determines whether something is or is not data science, cognitive psychology studies of relationships between language and concepts (e.g., Smith & Medin, 1981) tell us that it can be quite easy to break simple notions of what makes something belong or get excluded from being under a succinct label. Stated another way: even when we have words to refer to something, it does not guarantee we have clear boundaries for what that something is.[1]

Sometimes a term appears or begins to circulate and then gains rapid acceptance. That is the way of language and new words emerging, and this is how the meanings of words change. According to Cao (2017), one of the earliest uses of the term "data science" in academic publication was in 1974, in a book by Danish computer scientist Peter Naur. There, Naur defined it as "the science of dealing with data" with the assumption that data have been produced by someone else to be dealt with and what came after was the new science part. That certainly sounded reasonable, and was a fine term for his puposes, assuming that Naur was not dwelling on meeting the philosophical standards of what constitutes a science. Perhaps in some unwritten history, someone else uttered the words "data science", and it made an impression. Decades later, we use the term almost casually but then have some difficulty in explaining what the term means.

In other books and mentions of data science, there is often the use of a Venn diagram to convey what we talk about when we mention data science (Lee & Delaney, 2022). One frequently used one was published online by Drew Conway (2010), a computational social scientist who founded various data consulting groups. Conway's diagram has, since it has been posted on a blog, been shared, replicated, cited, and emulated ever since its debut in 2010. There are an extraordinary number of derivations and modified versions of the diagram—just run an image search on "data science venn diagram" and prepare to be impressed at all the ways people can riff on a relatively simple Venn diagram. In general, I acknowledge it has been embraced as a convenient way to give someone a sense of what we talk about when we say "data science", but still I hesitate to refer to it as definitive. The reason why I have hesitations on giving it definitive status is that under intense scrutiny, the diagram can raise many questions and get people tied up in knots in an effort to compactly characterize it and decide what exists specifically in different intersection points. Versions of this have been discussed in data science education commentaries such as one provided by Bill Finzer (2013), which also offers its own Venn diagram that is a bit less rigid on boundaries of what is and is not in data science. Versions of the Conway and Finzer versions are shown in Figure 2.1.

20 Advancing Data Science Education in K-12

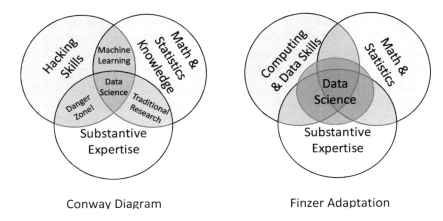

Figure 2.1 The Conway Venn diagram (left) showing a popular online depiction of what data science is, and an alternative version generated by William Finzer (right) that simplifies some of the same information of the Conway version.

However, Venn diagrams are controversial. Another objection that I have seen about the Conway diagram is expressed by Gould (2021), who specifically raised concerns about this depiction of data science with an educator and curriculum designer's perspective in mind:

> Venn diagrams fail to suggest the proportions of each discipline that exist in the intersection, and a naive reader might believe that data science consists of equal parts computer science, mathematics, and statistics, for example. Another natural misreading suggests that it is sufficient for students to engage in a comprehensive coverage of, for example, computer science, since such coverage would include the intersection of computer science with statistics and hence cover "data science".
>
> (P. S13)

These are valid points to raise when we think about what we teach, especially given a general constructivist epistemological orientation widely held in education and many pockets of developmental psychology that new knowledge comes into being by building upon what is already known. Other points of concern in the Venn diagram could be whether these are the right sets to highlight. For example, ethics does not appear, although as greater awareness of risks associated with data science that come from matters of privacy, social bias, and threats to individual agency would suggest ethical reasoning is really core to becoming a data scientist. Others still might challenge how much mathematics and statistics are bucketed together in these diagrams. And still others might challenge some of the labels given to certain intersection areas—such as the "danger zone" or the need for substantive disciplinary expertise. One could even ask what does this refer to in data science—are these three things that we expect a single individual to have? Or is it okay for a team to have different parts (one hacker, one statistical expert, and one field expert) and they work together? These pokes and prods can go on for a while, making it very difficult to accept the Conway Venn diagram or any of its derivatives as "the right one".

Also, while Conway is himself an accomplished and credentialed social scientist or perhaps what we would even call a data scientist, is his declaration the absolute authority for defining data science? Creating definitions, whether they are in a dictionary or *Wikpedia,* are large team efforts and undergo continual, although perhaps very gradual, revision. And if *Wikipedia* is any indication, there may not be agreement among all what is the actual definition even if one is offered and taken up by others. It also seems unusual to say, while acknowledging that Conway is an intelligent fellow and has thought carefully about what he shared, that over a decade later, we all look to a blog post as the definitive statement of the core of the subject or field.

So, with that in mind, let us consider some of the ways in which data science has been represented. One approach that follows is examining what seemingly authoritative texts represent as being data science. Another is to look at what people say and do when doing data science work, whether it is data scientists, commentators, or researchers who are studying data scientists in the field. I examine all of those in the sections below.

Data Science "by the book"

Textbooks and handbooks can be useful artifacts to examine when thinking about what was deemed important knowledge that should be organized in some way and passed down to others who are learning that field. However, as data science education is still emerging, it is hard to state what are the definitive texts. Keeping in mind that this is done for rhetorical purposes and not a systematic academic content analysis, I present some examples below. Partly, this was shaped by what was already on my bookshelf. But also, there is some additional informal rationale (which is also what led to those books ending up on my bookshelf in the first place).

For one pair of books, I look at ones published by *O'Reilly Media*. Those who have spent time in programming, information technology, and computer science may know those as the books that sport largely white covers and woodcut animal prints on the front as a signature feature. They are widely available in bookstores, and also I personally recall having to purchase some of these books in various college-level programming courses over time. Also, I will consider some of the authors and their status (again, this is an informal analysis).

In professional data science work, there is a notion of "tidy" data, frequently associated with Hadley Wickham, a New Zealand data scientist who produced some heavily used packages for data analysis and visualization in the *R* programming language. Briefly, data are "tidy" when, viewed as a table, every observation is a single row and each variable is a single column, and each cell only has one value in it. This common structure makes data easier to manipulate and visualize. Hadley Wickham and his advocacy for this have become well-known in professional data science communities. With co-author Garrett Grolemund—a software developer and Master Instructor for *RStudio* (an app that makes programming in R much friendlier with different panes to show the data and the code)—, Wickham released an *O'Reilly* book titled *R for Data Science* in 2017 (it has a woodcut of the kakapo, or owl parrot, on the cover for anyone who was wondering). The table of contents is provided in Table 2.1.

Table 2.1 Sections and chapters in Wickham and Grolemund's *R for Data Science*

R for Data Science by Hadley Wickham & Garrett Grolemund (2017) Table of contents	
Part 1: Explore	1. Data Visualization with *ggplot2*
	2. Workflow: Basics
	3. Data Transformation with *dplyr*
	4. Workflow: Scripts
	5. Exploratory Data Analysis
	6. Workflow: Projects
Part 2: Wrangle	7. Tibbles with *tibble*
	8. Data Import with *readr*
	9. Tidy Data with *tidyr*
	10. Relational Data with *dplyr*

(Continued)

Table 2.1 (Continued)

R for Data Science by Hadley Wickham & Garrett Grolemund (2017) Table of contents		
	11.	Strings with *stringr*
	12.	Factors with *forcats*
	13.	Dates and Times with *lubridate*
Part 3: Program	14.	Pipes with *magrittr*
	15.	Functions
	16.	Vectors
	17.	Iteration with *purr*
Part 4: Model	18.	Model Basics with *modelr*
	19.	Model Building
	20.	Many Models with *purrr* and *broom*
Part 5: Communicate	21.	R Markdown
	22.	Graphics for Communication with *ggplot2*
	23.	R Markdown Formats
	24.	R Markdown Workflow

There are a few things to note from this table of contents. The main overarching activities of data science, as represented in this book, are Explore, Wrangle, Program, Model, and Communicate (the different "Parts" in Table 2.1). Specific chapters cover R packages that can be used with tidy data (e.g., Chapter 1 in Table 2.1), with specific details for different types of data (dates and times vs text strings vs numerical values, Chapters 11 and 16, for example). Knowing those packages, which can be quite technical, is not important right now—but for anyone wondering, the packages are named with the unfamiliar sequences of letters or words that end in what seems like an extra "r". There is stuff early in the beginning about creating charts and data visualizations (Chapter 1). Also, there are some ways to organize the work of data science with workflows and pipes (e.g., Chapters 2, 4, 6, and 14) and using special commenting and organizing of code and prose (*R Markdown*, Chapter 21 onward). This seems to be a fairly technical book which involves pretty heavy programming work.

Let's consider another *O'Reilly Media* book, this time *Data Science from Scratch*, which is by Joel Grus and has a woodcut of a rock ptarmigan on the cover. Grus is a software engineer who previously worked at Google. One difference to know about this book is that it relies on *Python* as its programming language rather than R. The table of contents for this book is shown in Table 2.2.

Table 2.2 Chapters for Grus's *Data Science from Scratch*

Data Science from Scratch by Joel Grus (2019)
1. Introduction
2. A Crash Course in Python
3. Visualizing Data
4. Linear Algebra
5. Statistics
6. Probability
7. Hypothesis and Inference
8. Gradient Descent
9. Getting Data
10. Working with Data
11. Machine Learning
12. K-nearest Neighbors
13. Naïve Bayes
14. Simple Linear Regression
15. Multiple Regression
16. Logistic Regression
17. Decision Trees
18. Neural Networks
19. Clustering
20. Natural Language Processing
21. Network Analysis
22. Recommender Systems
23. Databases and SQL
24. MapReduce
25. Go Forth and Do Data Science

From Grus's table of contents, the topics look a bit more math and statistics focused in the early parts with content about linear algebra, statistics, probability, and hypothesis testing (Chapters 4–6). There is some stuff later in the book on simple linear, multiple, and logistic regression (Chapters 14–16) Then there are a number of specific techniques for optimization, classification, and modeling of data, including text data (Chapter 20). The book itself certainly has many pages of Python code intermixed with graphs and prose, but the math and statistics parts are a bigger emphasis in the Grus table of contents compared to the Wickham & Grolemund one. Between these two, the hacking and mathematics & statistics skills in the Conway Venn diagram feel pretty represented. If we consider the Conway diagram as a way[2] to think about this, we should also look at a book that represents substantive expertise—representing a specific domain or topic area for research. Because this current book is about K-12 education, let's take that as our substantive expertise topic and look at *Data Science in Education Using R* by Ryan A. Estrallado, Emily Freer, Jesse Mostipak, Joshua Rosenberg, and Isabella Velásquez (and yes, it is also on my bookshelf). This ensemble of authors represents a range of areas in education research and analysis and includes among them statisticians, educators, and a college professor. Being published by *Routledge* rather than *O'Reilly*, this book unfortunately does not have an animal woodcut on the cover but rather a number of colored pencils ordered in a way resembling a graph, evoking ideas about K-12 schools and data. Their table of contents is provided in Table 2.3.

Table 2.3 Chapters for Etrellado et al.'s *Data Science in Education Using R*

Data Science in Education Using R *by Ryan A. Estrellado, Emily A. Freer, Jesse Mostipak, Joshua M. Rosenberg, and Isabella C. Velásquez (2020)*

1. Introduction: Data Science in Education—You're Invited to the Party!
2. How to Use This Book
3. What Does Data Science in Education Look Like?
4. Special Considerations
5. Getting Started with *R* and *RStudio*
6. Foundational Skills
7. Walkthrough 1: The education data science pipeline with online science class data
8. Walkthrough 2: Approaching gradebook data from a data science perspective
9. Walkthrough 3: Using school level aggregate data to illuminate educational inequities
10. Walkthrough 4: Longitudinal analysis with federal students with disabilities data
11. Walkthrough 5: Text analysis with social media data
12. Walkthrough 6: Exploring social relationships using social network analysis with social media data
13. Walkthrough 7: The role (and usefulness) of multilevel models
14. Walkthrough 8: Predicting students' final grades using machine learning methods with online course data
15. Introducing data science tools to your education job
16. Teaching data science
17. Learning more
18. Additional resources
19. What Next

One thing to notice in this education-focused data science book is that aside from framing things as involving a "party" in the first chapter, the book is full of specific examples. The book contains eight walkthroughs (Chapters 7–14) that go through and use actual data sources, whether the data come from online course interactions, federal databases, or social media. The Estrallado et al. book addresses topics of concern to education researchers including inequities, social relationships, and test scores. Importantly, I do want to stress that there are some technical topics such as social network analysis (Chapter 12), multilevel models (Chapter 13), and machine learning (Chapter 14). This book, like Wickham and Grolemund's, is also using the programming language *R* and the *RStudio* environment. So while this book does not, on the basis of its table of contents, go into extensive detail about specific *R* packages, it is still doing things with mathematics and statistics and with programming but with an eye toward a specific domain (education, as a topic of study). The assumption seems to be that for education folks using this book, readers may not need to learn all the ins and outs of a specific *R* package in order to do some data science work on topics of interest.

Now looking across all three, there is not a lot of obvious chapter overlap. Network analysis appears in two out of three (Grus and Estrellado et al.), *R* appears in two (Wickham & Grolemund and Estrellado et al.) However, stating *R* is more essential to data science on the basis of it appearing in two books and *Python* is only in one is both inadequately supported by the data of three books' table of contents and also an easy way to get into an unwinnable argument between different camps of programming language enthusiasts. It is not completely clear that there is a really shared core to these from this casual look beyond the fact that all books involve data and all books involve some statistical programming. It is perhaps these three books are not comparable given they assume different levels, backgrounds, and interests and thus will be limited as far as helping us understand what is important for data science as a focus for students in K-12. Perhaps the next thing to do is to look at what is being taught in courses about data science and extrapolate from there.

Data Science "of Course"

Let us now consider what those who teach data science treat as data science by way of looking at the things they consider teaching. One course that has gained some notoriety at the college level and has made its contents widely available online is "Data 8: The Foundations of Data Science" offered at the University of California, Berkeley. As of 2024, this course is a requirement for data science majors at Berkeley. This course is referenced in the National Academies of Science, Engineering, and Medicine's consensus report (2018) on data science at the undergraduate levels and is mentioned several times as it is reflective of "well-packaged curriculum and materials" (p. 77). It can be found online at data8.org and is an introductory course—suggesting it does not expect an extensive prior background, yet it is considered a core part of data science.

Data 8 relies on online course materials and a number of specialized online tools that were prepared. It is taught every term (fall, winter, and summer) and traces back, online, to 2015. Because the course is taught by different instructors each term and has undergone some slight changes, I will focus just on one instance which was picked arbitrarily, although spot checks with other years and semesters suggest things look largely the same over time. The focal term is Summer 2022[3] (8 weeks in duration rather than 15 weeks, although the topics stay the same and are just done in larger blocks), and the overview of the course sequence is provided in Table 2.4, with some items such as holidays, exams, and review periods that are inherent parts of university-based courses removed for space.

Table 2.4 Syllabus Topics for Data 8 for Summer Term of 2022

Data 8 *as described on data8.org for Summer 2022 http://www.data8.org/su22/*	
Week 1	Cause and Effect
	Tables
	Data Types, Building Tables, Census
	Charts
Week 2	Functions
	Charts
	Histograms
	Conditionals and Iteration
	Groups, Pivots, and Joins
Week 3	Chance
	Sampling
	Models
	Comparing Distributions, Decisions and Uncertainty
Week 4	A/B Testing
	Causality

(Continued)

Table 2.4 (Continued)

Data 8 *as described on data8.org for Summer 2022* http://www.data8.org/su22/	
Week 5	Confidence Intervals
	Interpreting Confidence
	Center and Spread
	The Normal Distribution
	Sample Means, Designing Experiments
Week 6	Linear Regression
	Least Squares
	Residuals
	Regression Inference
Week 7	Classification
	Classifiers
	Updating Probabilities
	Advanced Prediction
Week 8	Privacy

Comparing this to the book table of contents above, Data 8 seems to be less about specific software (although it certainly involves programming) and emphasizes topics related to statistics, research methods, and a little bit on ethics (privacy). There is material about tables, charts, and histograms as well as general ideas like causality and models. It covers more topics than a high school Advanced Placement® (AP) statistics course and veers into machine learning activities like classification. It seems to emphasize a strong core understanding of ways that data are manipulated with computational tools and some foundational statistical and probability ideas along with guidance on how one can make inferences, groupings, and predictions. As a required introductory course for a college major that would likely have more advanced coursework on specialized topics, it seems to be accessible for a first-year major.

Perhaps we can shift our course gaze a little bit toward a younger set to things that are in K-12 classrooms. With Victoria Delaney, I have done this in an analysis of two self-identified data science curricula. One was *Introduction to Data Science* (IDS) (Gould et al., 2018), developed out of UCLA's Center X, and the other was *Bootstrap: Data Science* (B:DS) (Krishnamurthi et al., 2020). Both have data science in their names and have been implemented in many schools. *IDS* is intended for high school, whereas *B:DS* is for middle school and above. More about these two curricula is discussed in Chapter 4, and even more detail is in the original published study (Lee & Delaney, 2022). So, what are they covering when they teach data science?

The two curricula touch on, to different levels of depth, what data are; how we describe data using things like measures of center and data having distributional shapes; common visualizations like histograms and scatterplots; sampling from a population; a cycle of investigation with data called the data cycle; and some introductory machine learning (linear regression in both, decision trees and k-means clustering in *IDS*). Both involve some programming and programming activities (in *R* or *Pyret*, a language that has some similarities to *Python*). Of special interest is that *B:DS* really emphasizes good coding practice in terms of how to comment and thoroughly design and test computer functions. Ethics and famous cases of data being used in alarming ways are also in both curricula. There is a resemblance to topics found in a high school statistics course, although there is a bit more computational and programming focus in these two data science curricula. So, from the read of this, it seems like K-12 data science, as currently constructed, looks a bit like statistics but still involves some programming. These courses leave some intentional breadcrumbs for future work with machine learning. It also seems like these are foundations that will get students to more advanced and specialized tools and techniques like those in one of the books described above and depicted in Tables 2.1–2.3.

K-12 Data Science or Data Literacy?

The K-12 version of data science education, as currently instantiated, is looking less focused on specifics of programming and programming languages, heavily emphasizing statistics, and laying some basics about how to reason with and about data. It is quite common to observe this and then ask the question of whether K-12 data science is different from what we may just call "data literacy". How data literacy is even described among researchers is multifaceted (Gebre, 2022). Indeed, at a National Academies of Science, Engineering, and Medicine (NASEM) workshop convening experts to discuss the foundations of data science for students in grades K-12, this was an explicit question repeatedly raised by invited attendees (2023, p. 12). In response to this, statistics educator Robert Gould commented that this question was tied to a "false dichotomy between teaching data literacy and data science. Before teaching data science—and specific tools such as machine learning—students need a foundational understanding in data literacy" (NASEM, p. 12). He also expressed his own preference for a term that was put forward in the 2018 NASEM report on what we need for students to be fluent with data: data acumen.

Still, the usage of these terms "literacy" and "science" gets nebulous. On the one hand, Gould's description treats one ("data literacy") contributing to or comprising the foundation of the other ("data science"). To teach data literacy is doing some of the core work of teaching data science, although there is some very understandable ambiguity as the purpose of that convening was to identify where there were still confusions in education research. However, before offering my suggestions for how we can approach these data literacy vs data science questions, I do want to make an observation: The usage of these terms seems to go beyond semantics and can get loaded and imply power and status.

To illustrate this, consider that in January of 2024, the University of California convened a Board of Admissions and Relations with Schools (BOARS) workgroup to provide guidance on what mathematics courses offered in high schools would be considered as fulfilling specified admissions requirements. At the time, courses that self-identified as introductory for data science—including *IDS* above, for instance—had been at one point granted approval for fulfilling a specific university admissions requirement in place of Algebra 2 (a mathematics course that covers topics ranging from radicals, exponents, logarithms, polynomials, to inequalities). This had been a contentious matter, with parties having pretty different perspectives on what courses would contribute to student success in the future. Ultimately, where things stood at the time of this writing was that BOARS reviewed offerings and re-asserted that despite some precedent, currently offered high school data science courses did not meet the criteria for Algebra 2 substitution. In their comments[4] about those, the workgroup offered the following about three such courses: "we find these current courses labeled as 'data science' are more akin to data literacy courses" (Board of Admissions and Relations with Schools, 2024, p. 5).

What difference does this make? What does it mean to characterize courses to be about data literacy but not data science? In my interactions with literacy scholars, it seems pretty difficult to converge on full agreement on what we mean when we talk about literacy. For some in the reading and language arts community, it is fundamentally viewed as the ability to decode written text, as in learning phonics. Other, often described as "progressive", perspectives view it as a more complex social practice of meaning-making and cultural production and reproduction that is not exclusively bound to decoding of the literal "written word" and is quite messy when fully examined (Gee, 1989). These different emphases and beliefs on what is at the core of (reading) literacy have also gotten heated. In the 2020s, we are seeing the latest battle in "reading wars" where views on how to teach children to read are caricatured as being on either the phonics side or the whole language side. In fact, the use of "science" as a marker of power appears also in describing the research support for phonics-emphasizing approaches, dubbed "the science of reading" (see Duke & Cartwright, 2021, for some discussion of this). If the reading and use of text is our base referent for what we call literacy, and we are now trying to characterize *data* literacy, and the experts in reading literacy there are still having this disagreement, then it puts us in a messy position for figuring out what is data science and what is data literacy.

"Literacy" is a popular term that has been suggested a lot in education, but in other uses, it does not tend to cause such a stir. Sometimes we talk about media literacy, sometimes we talk about computational literacy (diSessa, 2000), and sometimes we talk about financial literacy. It has gotten to the point that when we classify something as a "literacy", it feels routine and not specialized. Concerns about teaching data literacy in place of data science, as voiced by some of the UC BOARS workgroup critiques, are coming from a well-intentioned place. Individuals who raise these concerns are themselves educators and data scientists. They are concerned because they are acutely aware that professional and college-level data science has a lot of complex things to it. To head toward data science means to commit in some way to meaningful engagement with those complex things, and the coursework should prepare for that. But at the same time, we need to consider how to reconcile observations made earlier in this chapter as we looked from professional resource texts (like Wickham & Grolemund (2017)) to things happening in K-12, which are seemingly sensible K-12 approaches to prepare for data science jobs in the future.

What might we do to better understand relationships, overlaps, and differences between what some people call data literacy and data science? I'll propose two sets of distinctions as an effort to clarify some things. One is to make more explicit how people are talking about the relationships between data literacy and data science when it comes to education and curriculum. I call those "fork, foundation, and infusion". The other set of distinctions will speak more to what different groups are foregrounding most when they advocate for data science. Those I call "data-science-as-process" and "data-science-as-content". I see those two sets of distinction to be ones that are not openly discussed but are at the core of some differences of opinions in the ongoing discussions about if and how data science education fits into our K-12 system.

Fork, Foundation, or Infusion

In the sections above, I have shared how there are ways in which data science and data literacy are talked about as separate and different from one another. It is a recurring question when presenting the idea of data science in K-12 education—which do we teach? Are they the same? Are they different? Does one rely on the other? At the core, I see this as people invoking different senses of the relationship between what we call data literacy and what we call data science.

I propose that moving forward, we think about three ways in which data literacy is being positioned relative to data science in current discourse: as a fork, foundation, or infusion. A diagram of this is shown in Figure 2.2, and here I summarize the distinctions. Note that, just as we can and do shift conceptions about the same thing if the situation necessitates (see Sherin et al., 2012), it is okay to lean on more than one of these ways of talking about the data literacy-science divide. It is not strictly belonging to one camp or the other. Some may feel firmly aligned with one view only. But there are also very smart people who in some situations talks about data literacy as a fork relative to data science may sometimes think of a data literacy/data science relationship that looks more like foundation or infusion approaches. It is rather a matter of when, in what contexts, and for what purposes.

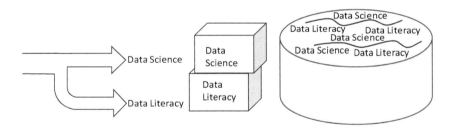

Figure 2.2 Data literacy positioned relative to data science in current discourse: as a fork, foundation, or infusion.

First, let's consider the fork. The most frequent suggestion that data literacy represents a different branch (or tine, I suppose) is when talking about educational trajectories. This has been prominent in the disagreements about mathematics instruction in California in the early to mid-2020s that accompanied debate about the 2023 California Mathematics Framework. Data literacy and courses that support that as their primary focus represent a different path for understanding and working with data than what is required in data science.

This is at the heart of the BOARS (2024) workgroup report. This seems to be one of the concerns among critics of self-identified high school data science courses (that are "more akin to data literacy") in California as this would be a path away from calculus or other mathematical subjects. According to that line of reasoning, this other path (the one that teaches data literacy) can be seen as less potent than or less representative of data science. Further, data science exists because of other mathematical ideas, such as those found in calculus and advanced algebra. Critics of the California Mathematics Framework (see some of the diverse set of rival commentaries in Boaler et al., 2024) suggest that sanctioning data literacy courses as a different pathway is going to steer students away from the requisite knowledge and proficiencies of data science but present itself to students incorrectly as being the path toward data science. A data science pathway to graduation in high schools is implying that students are becoming data scientists later, and the courses as they exist at the time, according to critics, do not support that path.

In this fork approach, data literacy of the sort as described by critics is fine to know but not designate as a specially sequenced high school foundations course. While knowing some basics about data, like specific measures and calculations, and how to read common visualization formats, may inherently be part of data science, these are proficiencies that are already part of earlier mathematics instruction. These are things students are supposed to learn in elementary and middle school. However, mathematics instructional time is limited and the amount that can go to statistical and data-related topics, while listed within standards, is limited. Informally speaking, data and statistics-related math topics are ones that can fall by the wayside in math classes when other parts of the math curriculum take longer than expected.

Shifting a bit away from debates about high school course sequences and the names of specific curricula or courses, another conception of data literacy in relation to data science is that data literacy is a foundation upon which data science relies. One must have data literacy in order to be effective as a data scientist. Given ongoing concerns about data literacy in the public—many people struggle with data (discussed more in the following chapter)—it may be that we really do need more data literacy overall. Not everyone needs to become a data scientist but everyone needs to be literate in data, whatever that means. As it stands, data literacy is not being adequately developed in K-8 instruction (such as for lack of time or it being dropped in a crowded curriculum or when it is taught, it is in need of new teaching approaches). However, in the foundation view, one must develop data literacy first as part of the cost of entry so that one may eventually pursue data science. Data literacy is a small portion of and essential base for what is ultimately needed to learn data science. This conception would welcome data literacy instruction as something all students should have, whether or not they opt to substantively pursue data science in the future.

The last conception I propose is that what we call data literacy is actually infused in data science to such a degree that it does not make sense to push hard for firm distinctions. Along this line of thinking, one could learn the names of specific algorithms, define optimization, and be able to complete some exercises that look like data science. However, if we look to the Conway Venn diagram, this is not a good place to land. To just know techniques but not understand what they mean or when they should be used for a given context is something of a "danger zone". A good data scientist is good because of the things we tend to call data literacy. Becoming good at data science means becoming good at those judgments and intuitions that data literacy should cover.

While recognizing that there are indeed some specialized tools and technologies for professional data science (remember cosine similarity?), there are still core ideas related to thinking about data and how to get information from them. There are also ideas that are so readily used with regularity (and even taught) in data science, like measures of center or measures of variability, common visualization types, and reflecting on the validity of some data for some question, that neither data literacy nor data science have a distinct claim on them.

This is acceptance of a fuzziness and inseparability between what we call data literacy and what we call data science, which can get some pushback. Some are tempted to argue that data science is a body of specialized stuff—very specific techniques, tools, and ideas—and needs its own distinction from less specialized stuff that is data literacy. Others may comfortably agree with the thinking of data literacy and data science as being in an infusion relationship. Along those lines, many who view this favorably see data science as largely a rebranding of the kinds of statistical thinking—which was a more formal way of referring to what people called data literacy. This raises another potential disagreement—not on what the relationship between the terms data literacy and data science is but rather in what we think of as even being the core or special stuff of data science.

Data-Science-as-Process and Data-Science-as-Content

Debates about what is the actual target of data science education—that is, what students learn when we say they learn data science—tend to require wrestling with dual emphases on process and on content as they relate to the work of data scientists. My observation from watching these debates is that some characterizations of what constitutes the core of data science favor one side over the other, although there are ways in which we genuinely care about both. Ultimately, these process and content conversations should not be thought of as exclusionary. However, I will talk about them separately in order to better express what is associated with data-science-as-process and what is associated with data-science-as-content emphases, even though process and content are ultimately intimately connected. It just depends on what topics are implied as being distinctive content.

When we emphasize data-science-as-process, we are emphasizing what people do in order to investigate and interpret data. What makes for a savvy data scientist, regardless of what specific domain or professional context, is the ability to follow data inquiries. This involves, but is not limited to, careful interrogations and posing of core questions that can be answered with data. The questions might relate to the overall investigation—such as what other products people tend to buy after purchasing *CleansSoWell* detergent or whether there is indeed an effect on public health as a result of changing levels of air pollutants across decades. Teaching data-science-as-process stresses teaching students to reflect on what is represented in a set of data and helping them understand how we go about interacting with and manipulating that data to gain insight. The goal is for students to make inferences and discoveries, to tell stories with and about data, and to raise justified critiques about analysis and inferences.

Versions of a process emphasis have appeared in various guidance documents and early K-12 data science curricula. One document of importance in statistics education, and increasingly in conversations about data science education, is the *GAISE II* report from the American Statistical Association (Bargagliotti et al., 2020). *GAISE* stands for *Guidance for Assessment and Instruction in Statistics Education*. A first *GAISE* report was released in 2005 with some revisions in 2007 (Franklin et al., 2007). The more recent *GAISE* report, known as *GAISE II* and released in 2020, was authored by a committee of experienced statisticians and statistics educators who have direct experience with data science. It is a carefully developed resource that describes three levels of competence (known as Levels A, B, and C) that should build upon one another, although by design the report does not give explicit prescriptions of what should be mastered by what grade level the way that standards documents tend to do. The *GAISE II* report also provides examples of the kinds of things that students should be able to do at each level with sample investigations and data. For example, the ability to describe data collected about ladybugs or bean growth would be part of Level A. Level B might involve making comparisons across data on Galapagos Finches as observed by Darwin, and Level 3 could involve inferring associations between different variables such as the effect of light on radish seedlings or puzzling over whether there is a relationship between napping and heart attacks. See the *GAISE II* report for more details and for these examples.

GAISE II is very process-oriented. It establishes a "Statistical problem-solving *process*" [emphasis added] framework and explicitly names four components at the core of the process. Those components include:

I. Formulate statistical investigative questions
II. Collect/consider the data
III. Analyze the data
IV. Interpret the results

GAISE II mentions, but does not stress, specific algorithms or content outside of the ability to demonstrate mastery over those process components. This report was informed by frameworks that had come out of the statistics education research community, including one called PPDAC articulated by Wild and Pfannkuch (1999) in a review of literature and interviews with statisticians. PPDAC stands for:

- Problem—formulate a statistical question
- Plan—figure out what data are needed and how to get it
- Data—collect, manage, clean, and organize the data
- Analysis—explore the data and visualize it to get relevant information
- Conclusion—answer the statistical question and provide reasoning

And a version of process emphasis that bears resemblance to these investigative processes is the data cycle, which is an explicit part of the *Introduction to Data Science* and *Bootstrap: Data Science* curricula. The four components of the data cycle are similar to the frameworks above (and especially the *GAISE II*), but the specific components are as follows: Ask Questions, Consider Data, Analyze Data, and Interpret Data (see Figure 2.3). One could dig in further on why there are slightly different versions in these documents and think about ease of expressing these different components, but the important feature across all of these is that they are emphasizing processes. Data science work, extending what has been done in statistical inquiry but with some newer tools, is fundamentally investigative work and ways of thinking about questions, data, and interpretations.

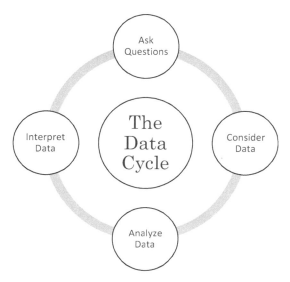

Figure 2.3 Depiction of the data cycle.

A data-science-as-process emphasis would be more agnostic with respect to what are the tools and systems that should be used in the process of gathering and analyzing data. If one were to collect a survey of thousands of people by hand outside of a supermarket, those data would be valid and acceptable for use in data science. It would also be fine if this were a set of online surveys, or perhaps instead of surveys, then recorded clicks or sensor values. These are all fine collections of data, and, in principle, a good data scientist should be capable of conducting inquiry with any of these data and be able to do so in a range of high- and low-tech scenarios.

Of course, computers help especially when there are large numbers or many calculations involved, but whether one uses R or *Python* or C++ or *Matlab* or *Microsoft Excel* or a scientific calculator does not particularly matter beyond efficiency and risk of computational errors. The data-science-as-process emphasis is broadly accepting of the idea that the tools of the moment will change, new programming languages will emerge, tools that do what programmers can do but do not require users to be fluent in the programming languages will emerge (like *ChatGPT* or *GitHub Copilot*), and our technical capabilities will adapt as society and technology change. Thus, it is unclear whether the cost of learning a particular programming language or tool system with a high learning overhead is worth it when the hallmark abilities to do data science are in the ability to responsibly enact or contribute to the processes of data science. This does not mean that teaching of programming is unnecessary, but rather some treatments of data-science-as-process will favor computational thinking over stressing mastery of specific languages.

Let's turn now to a data-science-as-content emphasis. While processes require content and content is only meaningful in use, a caricature of content emphasis is that content is "the things that one should know". While there is melding of process and content, current Common Core Math Standards[5] (National Governors Association, 2010) have embodiments of content emphasis (and the specific standards that provide this emphasis have the word "content" as part of their name). Some examples from the Common Core for sixth grade mathematics:

- CCSS.MATH.CONTENT.6.SP.B.5
- Summarize numerical data sets in relation to their context, such as by:
    - CCSS.MATH.CONTENT.6.SP.B.5.A
    - Reporting the number of observations.
    - CCSS.MATH.CONTENT.6.SP.B.5.B
        Describing the nature of the attribute under investigation, including how it was measured and its units of measurement.
    - CCSS.MATH.CONTENT.6.SP.B.5.C
        Giving quantitative measures of center (median and/or mean) and variability (interquartile range and/or mean absolute deviation), as well as describing any overall pattern and any striking deviations from the overall pattern with reference to the context in which the data were gathered.
    - CCSS.MATH.CONTENT.6.SP.B.5.D
        Relating the choice of measures of center and variability to the shape of the data distribution and the context in which the data were gathered.

In this Common Core example, specific "things to know" include units of measurement, measures of center (such as the median and mean) and measures of variability (including the interquartile range and mean absolute deviation), and features of data such as shape of a distribution. These are by no means useless things to know, but there are certain topics, algorithms, and terms as well as how they relate to one another clearly specified.

Those Common Core standards are presented in terms of measurement, statistics, data, and probability. Certainly, these are important for data science, but one might object that data science is different even from those areas of content because they involve even more specialized ideas. Indeed, these seem to be the topics that one sees in a guidebook or syllabus (see Tables 2.1–2.4 for reference). For instance, mastery of data science content could involve knowing a breadth of clustering algorithms, being able to define gradient descent, and being able to explain the differences between precision and recall. It could also be knowledge about specific programming languages and tools, such as *Jupyter Notebooks* or the *R* programming language and valued libraries or packages. While being able to think effectively with data, one could argue that the reality of data science practice is that the work we do requires use of specific tools; a young data scientist who does not know how to use a notebook (like *Jupyter Notebooks*) or install a useful *R* package would likely struggle, even if they know what processes are involved in investigation. For specific subject areas and fields, there may be even more specific content demands. Knowing the measurements of pollution density or why logarithmic scales are used in some analyses are important for different fields and problems.

Also, this supports an argument for Algebra 2 and Calculus content as an important requirement for future data science education. It is important to know about partial derivatives, exponential and polynomial expressions, n-dimensional space, cosine similarity (there it is!), and integrals in order to fully grasp how specific algorithms work or how to optimize under specific situations. At question here is for those who foreground data-science-as-content, what content are they treating as distinctive. For some, it is machine learning, artificial intelligence, and specific mathematical ideas that are reflected in topics like calculus. For others, it is content that is broadly useful for many varieties of data work, such as specific types of visualizations, measurements, and properties of aggregated data. However, in the current educational system, those bits of broad-use content are learned but not necessarily learned well in the context of use. This makes data-science-as-process more important to teach in order to give that broad-use content meaning and purpose. Thus, data-science-as-content is typically reflective of new specialized topics (e.g., machine learning). Unless otherwise stated, data-science-as-content will be referring to those specialized emphases more than the broad-use topics.

Where there appear to be tensions and disagreements is when someone feels that data-science-as-process or data-science-as-content (remember: this is implying the specialized topics, like cosine similarity) are being de-emphasized in advocacy for data science education. A fervent data-science-as-process advocate could argue that any grade level can and should learn the investigative process and how to think carefully about data, whether the data are about how many kids in the class have brown hair or if one is analyzing complex clickstream data from a website. A fervent data-science-as content advocate could argue that unless someone knows the mathematics of change or matrix operations, they have not broached the core of data science. However, both data-science-as-process and data-science-as-content are important and in different ways and at different times. I do contend, however, that this is partly driving distinctions between fork, foundation, and infusion conversations about data science and data literacy. A fork would steer students away from data-science-as-content topics that may include things like calculus that may be relevant to data science. A foundation would require some ideas—such as inequalities—be established in order to access others—such as integrals. An infusion would not necessarily see there being clean distinctions because the process matters and is connected to all manners of content that is broadly usable and likely to change over time and with advances in technology. It tends to be less committed to specific data-science-as-content topics, not because they are not useful nor interesting but because they are subject to change and needs for specific disciplines or data problem types.

Data Science "On the Job"

If we struggle so much in stating what is data science and what distinguishes it, there are still other approaches we could take beyond the review of books and courses above. One might be able to just look at job listings for the role of data scientist or official descriptions such as what is provided by the Bureau of Labor Statistics (BLS). Certainly, every employer will differ on exact requirements based on what technology infrastructure they use and what kinds of problems they solve. However, some responsibilities that one can find easily by searching the ads for data scientist positions will include—at least in 2024—using analytics, coding with *Python* or *R*, querying databases, and knowing statistical approaches to working with data. And in business, it is not at all uncommon to see that there are responsibilities like collaborating with teams, managing personnel and projects, and communicating with clients or other organizational units. The BLS, which has projected the third largest increase for future job growth (see Chapter 1), offers a very succinct definition of what the work is: "Data scientists use analytical tools and techniques to extract meaningful insights from data".

Well, that BLS description left some things unspecified. So, looking at general descriptions about jobs might only get us so far. Perhaps surveys of data scientists could help? I have mentioned elsewhere that Kaggle (kaggle.com) is one important online community and repository for data scientists in that it provides data sets, challenges, and online discussion communities. The 2022 Kaggle Data Science & ML [Machine Learning] Survey[6] obtained responses from 23,997 respondents across 173 countries. Now, it is important to consider that surveys require some thoughtful consideration—not all data scientists use Kaggle nor do they all complete surveys, so representativeness and generalizability should not be assumed by default. However, with those caveats, the results of Kaggle's survey suggest *Python* and *SQL* are the most commonly used programming languages. However, *C* and *C++* are also still represented. (Does this mean if we want to teach data-science-as-content we should be teaching *C* and *C++?*). *Jupyter Notebooks* is used by over 80% of respondents but there are over 20% using *RStudio*, and still some people using *Matlab*. Cloud computing matters to many although there are three large rivals who have shares of users (Amazon Web Services, Google Cloud Platform, and Microsoft Azure). From that, we glean that there are specific programming languages and tools that are used, but do not have much information in the way of using statistics as part of data scientific work.

While not a systematic survey, there is also frequently mention among data scientists of the "80/20" rule among data scientists whereby 80% of the work involves gathering and cleaning the data (e.g., getting rid of empty values, standardizing measures, making things "tidy") to be used in analysis and the other 20% actually doing analysis. This is not based on an actual academic research study on time use, but rather lore that has been broadly accepted and gets communicated in many data science college lectures and by professionals. Data science graduate students around me conducting research would also attest to this as accurate (although some might even claim it is more than 80% time spent dealing with data rather than analyzing it), and accompany that statement with groans and other expressions of frustration. From their experience and my own, data cleaning takes a lot of time and is a lot of work!

Okay, having at least considered some other sources, let's look at some research. One study I like a lot is by Hollylynne Lee and colleagues (Lee et al., 2022) and was a phenomenological study of data scientists. For this study, Lee immersed herself for nine months in 2018–2019 with *RTI International*, a research institute that handles many data-intensive projects. This work included observations, field notes, interviews, and cross-checking with the observed data scientists to confirm or refine any interpretations made by the research team. The team also did interviews with data scientists in other organizations in industry and non-profit work.

Lee et al. (2022) found that data scientists considered statistics and computational fluency to be important, but participants commented that either or both could be learned on the job by motivated individuals. While languages like *Python*, *R*, and *SQL* were used along with *Excel* and *GitHub*, flexibility was necessary. Data scientists used multiple tools and many would need to create their own for specific purposes. They were thoughtful about data that they typically received from a third party and asked what the data did and did not represent and if biases could be introduced (sort of like the mention above that Kaggle surveys do not necessarily represent all data scientists because not all data scientists use Kaggle). Communication and storytelling, as data scientists frequently show their findings to others and explain their work, were also important. They needed to be able to help others understand what was actionable information and on what grounds certain interpretations could be made. They had to rely on their own careful consideration of the data and personal curiosity to develop robust understandings and anticipate questions that they received when communicating about their work to others in and out of their organizations.

The descriptions Lee et al. formulated and confirmed with the data scientists they had studied emphasized key features of data-science-as-process.

> The data scientists did not blindly apply data analytic techniques. Instead, they worked on developing a deep understanding of the problem and context that encompassed a project or needs of a client. They were immersed in context throughout a project and always had an eye towards the value of their work for clients, business, or a discipline.
>
> (p. 9)

Data scientists explored data, whether it was a raw format or in exploratory visualizations. They also ran simulations and built statistical models with an awareness of uncertainty being an inherent feature of those models. Ultimately, from this empirical work and from a review of existing literature, Lee et al. proposed a framework for what data science involves that is process-oriented and includes similar components to those documented elsewhere (e.g., Bargagliotti et al., 2020; Wild & Pfannkuch, 1999) with some specific modifications. Lee et al.'s framework includes

- Frame the Problem—Understand the context being studied and pose an appropriate question with some possible strategies for answering it

- Consider & Gather Data—Know the qualities of the data including size, variables, methods used to get the data, and trustworthiness as they relate to the problem at hand
- Process Data—Clean the data and organize it in ways amenable to analysis and consider additional data to combine with it
- Explore & Visualize Data—Get descriptive information like statistical measures and produce visualizations to show the data in order to get a sense of possible relationships that may be uncovered through further analysis
- Consider Models—Analyze and identify possible models and modeling techniques that could be used with the data and what assumptions and limitations are associated with those
- Communicate and Propose Action—Prepare a story about the data to convey important ideas to a stakeholder audience and be prepared to make recommendations and provide justifications with awareness of limitations in the approach and data

Importantly, these processes were part of a cycle that would feed into itself and with the different components bleeding into each other.

So, the picture we get about professionals does include aspects of process and content and both general and specific competencies. Statistical and computational proficiencies matter, but there are no discrete knowledge bodies or definite platforms that obviously dominate data science in the workplace—rather, there are ensembles of tools and systems that can do a range of things, and data scientists have to be able to know what they want to get and be comfortable looking at data and understanding how we can use computers to help us make sense of data but in ways that have inherent limits to them. That is, by teaching someone *R* and Amazon Web Services plus k-means clustering, we have not yet necessarily made ourselves a ready-to-work data scientist. Those specific tools and techniques are not obviously the core requirement for things to teach in K-12 data science. At the same time, while we can stress processes and help people to appreciate that data require careful reflection and require us to use a range of techniques such as visualization and modeling, we will only get so far if those individuals only know those techniques exist but cannot directly use them themselves. The professional work of data science involves not just knowing that these things matter, but how to do them as well, with the expectation that even the most current tools and techniques are going to change and it will require hacks and creative manipulations to do the work that data scientists need to get done.

The Data Science "Sniff Test"

Here is one other way of thinking about what data science and data science education that has gotten some uptake. Tim Erickson is a longtime contributor to statistics education research and what is emerging as data science education. His offering to a definition is not rigid with respect to specific tools or specific content. It is resonant with interest in data-science-as-process. Erickson questions whether data-science-as-content delineations—such as professional data science as defined by knowledge of advanced machine learning techniques—are appropriate ones to make. There are some qualities, however, that seem to recur in conversations about what happens in data science work, and those are the reference point for his data science education "sniff test" (Erickson, 2020). He proposes focusing on the degree to which something "smells" like data science.

Erickson's sniff test has two major components, which I summarize from his writings (Erickson, 2020) but also having been in conversations with him and hearing him speak very thoughtfully on the topic. Effectively, the two components of his sniff test are, from the student's perspective:

- *Feeling awash with data*—the amount of data is large enough and has enough attributes that it would be impractical to just use brute force hand calculation or manual graphing to work with it. This means having five numbers to work with will not emit a strong "data science scent", but having at least several dozen or perhaps even hundreds or thousands would make the task feel like the tools of computation are good ones to use.
- *Knowing that "data moves" are necessary to get insights*—The information one might glean from the data is not obvious in the current form, and there is work one must do in order to have a sense of what is going on in the data and, more specifically, answer a question that you have or are going to be generating. He has talked about this in terms of "Data moves" (Erickson et al., 2019) being required, with data moves being acceptably thought of as operations on data such as filtering, sorting, grouping, or calculating.

Also, to stay consistent with other aspects of documented work of data scientists (Lee et al., 2022), although it is not necessarily as essential, Tim emphasizes the need to communicate about the data. This invites the need to create visualizations that can make certain ideas more visible to others and to be equipped to tell the story about or hidden within the data to other people. It is not an essential part of the sniff test, but it can certainly enhance resemblance to what we know data scientists must frequently do.

This means that while writing computer code, using libraries like *pandas* or *dplyr*, or cleaning data might be the type of thing that one does in a professional data scientist job or in the work of advanced academic research that uses data science. However, those libraries or activities add to but do not in and of themselves inherently define the scent of data science. A student using a drag-and-drop tool or even *Microsoft Excel* could be doing something that indeed smells like data science, according to the Erickson sniff test. The sniff test gives us one way to think about data science education having legitimacy in its K-12 forms. Given that educational software tools often work to address some unique challenges for learners—by including scaffolding (Pea, 2004) and providing students with ways to get acquainted with important ideas without being hindered by things like reading level, prior coding experience, or inherent time constraints that come with being in a classroom that has many other things to cover as well—it allows us to think broadly about ways to do data science across ages.

Data Science for the Rest of This Book

Having covered a number of ways to consider how we define or conceptualize what data science is, and therefore what data science education is, readers may wonder what is the position taken through this book. For the purposes of this book, and the subsequent chapters, I will be using the term data science generously and with data-science-as-process implied, although there will inevitably be contact with some ideas that are pertinent to content that is broad-use. This means that when we teach *practices* and *ways of thinking* that are deeply supportive of data science investigation, like helping students to recognize how and when it is useful to describe a distribution of data or when a student gains proficiency in making informal or statistical data-based inferences, we are doing data science education. This appears to be the direction of K-12 data science education efforts and is supported by documents like *GAISE II* (Bargogliotti et al., 2020). Also, in education and education research, we often view learning as cyclical, refined over future cycles, and based on prior knowledge that comes from things learned and experienced both in and out of classrooms. Early work with data graphs in elementary school then is valid as part of data science education even though more work in later K-12 years may still be required in order to specialize and increase what one knows or can do with different data visualization types. In postsecondary and in professional practice, this could get even more advanced or novel.

This is foundation-like (see earlier fork, foundation, and infusion section) in that new ideas will build upon earlier ones, but I would maintain there are fundamental infusion qualities to this view. Getting information from data visualizations, for instance, is so pervasive and core to data science work that we have little to gain in treating that activity as separable into things that one does only for data literacy or only for data science. Granted, taking that visualization example further, there may be some specific forms that get used a lot, such as histograms or scatterplots. However, that does not mean that other forms are less important or that advanced data science has sole ownership of those and data literacy has others.

Also, to make this way of viewing data science and data science education feel more comfortable, we can consider analogies for how we talk about learning in other subjects. It is fine to say young kids do science at school. For example, a middle school student can be doing chemistry when participating in a well-designed class activity making soap from lard and lye. That is something we say without hesitation or excessive deliberation. In saying that the student is doing chemistry, we have a common understanding that we are not asserting that by making soap in class (e.g., McNeill & Krajcik, 2008) that student is immediately ready to use a mass spectrometer or is going immediately into a pharmaceutical lab right after class. We know that will require more advanced work, with more coursework and more to learn ahead. Similarly, I do not see a problem with saying a fifth grader is doing data science and not inferring from that that the same fifth grader is ready to jump into the data science team for consumer products at Google. Following Wise (2020), there can be use and benefit in thinking about students as preparing to be "data scientists". It would, however, be misleading to think of or provide data science education as a fork that disconnects from other important ideas and experiences that could be very useful for future data science work. At present, we should not expect nor present a single high school data science course as being enough on its own to fully equp a youth to do data science professionally. But we can have rich experiences in such a course that will be helpful and additive toward becoming a data scientist down the road, along with other courses and preparation experiences that already exist.

This view also means that while computation is important in data science, we have ways of helping students to learn data science that do not immediately rely on a computers or programming. Computers and programming can certainly help, but we can still appreciate that there are ways to learn important computational ideas both in front of and away from a keyboard, touchscreen, or mouse. Even better is when we find ways to really help students to make those connections between learning an important computational idea in an analog way and how to think about that idea with digital tools as well.

Recognizing activities that may sound "basic" as part of data science education also does not exclude things that may sound "advanced"—topics that tend to be the purview of data-science-as-content (recall: this is in reference to the specialized content). Say we consider machine learning to be "advanced". There are exciting new ways to teach ideas related to machine learning to K-12 students (e.g., Shapiro & Fiebrink, 2019). For example, Google's *Teachable Machine* (Carney et al., 2020) does not require user knowledge of linear algebra in order to understand how classification works. Those are certainly worthwhile to explore, and they are part of data science education as well. They are not, however, the entirety nor the pre-requisite for getting started.

For a relatively new field that changes as our technical capabilities and societal needs change, there will be some instability in data science—but this is also why we do things like revisit and refine standards, create new curriculum, and regularly ask what is important for students to learn now and toward what ends. Things that are important "to-dos" for the future for data science education will be to articulate standards and progressions for learning, with the hope that some terminology introduced here (e.g., data-science-as-process, data-science-as-content) can help in conversations, as well as demonstrate more what this can look like in the classroom. The classroom and types of data science education experiences that appear in the literature are the focus of a later chapter (Chapter 4). Most immediately, I will turn to what we know already about how people think about and learn data. This can help us to appreciate that data science education is something that will require work and concerted effort because thinking with data as data science requires us to do is not an inherently simple thing for humans to do.

Notes

1 Consider, for instance, that single words can have different senses, different meanings, and contexts of use. And one additional example to consider for how difficult definition can be is the quote made famous by US Supreme Court Justice Potter Stewart in determining what counts as obscenity/pornography: "I know it when I see it".

2 Note that I did not say it is *the* way
3 http://www.data8.org/su22/.
4 The link to the report is available at https://senate.universityofcalifornia.edu/_files/committees/boars/documents/boarsacwphase1report-20240221.pdf.
5 see https://www.thecorestandards.org/Math/.
6 https://www.kaggle.com/kaggle-survey-2022.

References

Bargagliotti, A., Franklin, C., Arnold, P., Gould, R., Johnson, S., Perez, L., & Spangler, D. (2020). *Pre-K-12 Guidelines for Assessment and Instruction in Statistics Education (GAISE) report II*. Alexandria, VA: American Statistical Association and National Council of Teachers of Mathematics.

Boaler, J., Conrad, B., Ford, B., Mazzeo, R., & Nelson, J. (2024). Three views on the California math framework. *Notices of the American Mathematical Society, 71*(6), 797–805. https://doi.org/10.1090/noti2957

Board of Admissions and Relations with Schools (BOARS). (2024). *Statement on mathematics (Area C) admissions requirements*. Retrieved from Oakland, CA: https://senate.universityofcalifornia.edu/_files/committees/boars/documents/boarsacwphase1report-20240221.pdf

Cao, L. (2017). Data science: A comprehensive overview. *ACM Computing Surveys (CSUR), 50*(3), Article 43. https://doi.org/10.1145/3076253

Carney, M., Webster, B., Alvarado, I., Phillips, K., Howell, N., Griffith, J., … Chen, A. (2020). *Teachable machine: Approachable web-based tool for exploring machine learning classification*. Paper presented at the Extended Abstracts of the 2020 CHI Conference on Human Factors in Computing Systems, Honolulu, HI. https://doi.org/10.1145/3334480.3382839

Conway, D. (2010). The data science venn diagram. Retrieved from https://doi.org/10.1145/3076253

diSessa, A. A. (2000). *Changing minds: Computers, learning, and literacy*. Cambridge: MIT Press.

Duke, N. K., & Cartwright, K. B. (2021). The science of reading progresses: Communicating advances beyond the simple view of reading. *Reading Research Quarterly, 56*(S1), S25–S44. https://doi.org/10.1002/rrq.411

Erickson, T. (2020). *Awash in data: An introduction to data science with CODAP*. Retrieved from https://concord.org/awash-in-data

Erickson, T., Wilkerson, M., Finzer, W., & Reichsman, F. (2019). Data moves. *Technology Innovations in Statistics Education, 12*(1). Retrieved from https://escholarship.org/uc/item/0mg8m7g6

Estrellado, R. A., Freer, E., Rosenberg, J. M., & Velásquez, I. C. (2020). *Data science in education using R*. London: Routledge.

Finzer, W. (2013). The data science education dilemma. *Technology Innovations in Statistics Education, 7*(2). Retrieved from https://escholarship.org/uc/item/7gv0q9dc

Franklin, C., Kader, G., Mewborn, D., Moreno, J., Peck, R., Perry, M., & Scheaffer, R. (2007). *Guidelines for assessment and instruction in statistics education (GAISE) report: A pre-k–12 curriculum framework*. Alexandria, VA: American Statistical Association.

Gebre, E. (2022). Conceptions and perspectives of data literacy in secondary education. *British Journal of Educational Technology, 53*(5), 1080–1095. https://doi.org/10.1111/bjet.13246

Gee, J. P. (1989). What is literacy. *Journal of Education, 171*(1), 18–25.

Gould, R. (2021). Toward data-scientific thinking. *Teaching Statistics, 43*(S1), S11–S22. https://doi.org/10.1111/test.12267

Gould, R., Machado, S., Johnson, T. A., & Molynoux, J. (2018). *Introduction to Data Science v 5.0*. Los Angeles, CA: UCLA Center X.

Grus, J. (2019). *Data science from scratch: First principles with python*. Sebasatopol, CA: O'Reilly Media.

Krishnamurthi, S., Schanzer, E., Politz, J. G., Lerner, B. S., Fisler, K., & Dooman, S. (2020). Data science as a route to AI for middle-and high-school students. *arXiv preprint arXiv:2005.01794*.

Lee, H., Mojica, G., Thrasher, E., & Baumgartner, P. (2022). Investigating data like a data scientist: Key practices and processes. *Statistics Education Research Journal, 21*(2).

Lee, V. R., & Delaney, V. (2022). Identifying the content, lesson structure, and data use within pre-collegiate data science curricula. *Journal of Science Education and Technology, 31*, 81–98. https://doi.org/10.1007/s10956-021-09932-1

McNeill, K. L., & Krajcik, J. (2008). Scientific explanations: Characterizing and evaluating the effects of teachers' instructional practices on student learning. *Journal of Research in Science Teaching, 45*(1), 53–78. https://doi.org/10.1002/tea.20201

National Academies of Sciences, Engineering, and, & Medicine. (2018). *Data science for undergraduates: Opportunities and options*. Washington, DC: National Academies Press.

National Academies of Sciences, Engineering, and Medicine. (2023). *Foundations of data science for students in grades K-12: Proceedings of a workshop*. Washington, DC: The National Academies Press.

National Governors Association. (2010). *Common core state standards*. Washington, DC: National Governors Association.

Naur, P. (1974). *Concise survey of computer methods*. Lund, Sweden: Studentlitteratur.

Pea, R. D. (2004). The social and technological dimensions of scaffolding and related theoretical concepts for learning, education, and human activity. *The Journal of the Learning Sciences, 13*(3), 423–451. Retrieved from https://www.jstor.org/stable/1466943

Shapiro, R. B., & Fiebrink, R. (2019). Introduction to the special section: Launching an agenda for research on learning machine learning. *ACM Transactions on Computing Education, 19*(4), Article 30. https://doi.org/10.1145/3354136

Sherin, B., Krakowski, M., & Lee, V. R. (2012). Some assembly required: How scientific explanations are constructed in clinical interviews. *Journal of Research in Science Teaching, 49*(2), 166–198. https://doi.org/10.1002/tea.20455

Smith, E. E., & Medin, D. L. (1981). *Categories and concepts*. Cambridge, MA: Harvard University Press.

Wickham, H., & Grolemund, G. (2017). *R for data science: Import, tidy, transform, visualize, and model data*. Sebastopol, CA: O'Reilly Media, Inc.

Wild, C. J., & Pfannkuch, M. (1999). Statistical thinking in empirical enquiry. *International Statistical Review, 67*(3), 223–248. https://doi.org/10.1111/j.1751-5823.1999.tb00442.x

Wise, A. F. (2020). Educating data scientists and data literate citizens for a new generation of data. *Journal of the learning sciences, 20*(1), 164–181. https://doi.org/10.1080/10508406.2019.1705678

Humans Thinking about Data

3

For right now, let's follow a tendency to think of data as being represented by a lot with numbers. (Data can take many forms, but numbers and graphs are frequently recognized as relating to data. Ask an artificial intelligence (AI) image generator to show an image of data or run an image search online, and this becomes apparent, at least for people who contribute content on the internet.) If humans tended to already be good at working with numerical data, we probably would not need to worry so much about the need to teach how to reason with it. However, the evidence does not seem to support people being innately data savvy. For one, statistics and data analysis techniques are relatively recent inventions in documented intellectual human history (Wiggins & Jones, 2023). It is pretty hard to be adept with a set of tools that had not been formally established.

It is worth appreciating also that while there are some very impressive properties of mathematics and what it helps us understand, there are a lot of different ways people have had to develop ways of representing and doing the number stuff of math. For example, we often use a base-10 system (ostensibly, having ten fingers is helpful in that regard), but that is not the basis of all cultural groups counting systems (e.g., see Saxe's (1991) discussion of the body number system documented among the Oksapmin people and how larger cultural changes affected ways that number system was used). When telling time, we use different bases (60, 12, 24). Zero was "invented" or discovered thousands of years ago in Babylonia or India (Seife, 2000), or perhaps in Mesoamerica by Mayans (Batz, 2021). The point here is that while we can see and use numbers everywhere, there are innovations in history that had to be created—and as we create new things, we need to learn how to use those.

DOI: 10.4324/9781003385264-3

So the idea that numerical data—the purview of a lot of statistics—and probabilistic uncertainty—can be hard for people is not difficult to understand. In evolutionary terms, counting to 1,000 probably did not have great benefit, and it requires added work to learn and appreciate since human brains were not dealing with that as a survival need (Feigenson et al., 2004).

This chapter summarizes some of the known challenge areas documented with respect to learning things about data and data science. Whether these have biological or cultural bases (or both) is not discussed here as that merits other investigations. Also, other sources like mathematics education and mathematical cognition handbooks have good details about numeracy, proportional reasoning, and other things that speak to numbers and operations that are not necessarily tied to data. Data (as the topic of interest to learn) are this book's focus, which points us to work in cognitive psychology, statistics education research, and other fields. First, I share some generally known difficulties and tendencies that have appeared in the literature regarding reasoning with and about data. Then I focus more specifically on findings and ideas from statistics education.

Reasoning under Uncertainty with Heuristics

Some classic examples of how humans reason (with difficulty) include classic work on probabilistic and statistical reasoning most often associated with Daniel Kahneman and Amos Tversky. There is a tendency for humans to rely on some tricks that can help them make quick decisions and judgments, but in a world where we accrue numbers and use them as data, we are susceptible to producing errors. In his book *Thinking Fast and Slow*, Kahneman (2011) expressed this as part of the challenges between fast thinking done by one reasoning system (called System 1) and when we are more deliberative and can take more time to puzzle through something (using something called System 2). Much of the work, including that which led to Kahneman receiving the Nobel Prize, was done in collaboration with Amos Tversky who preceded him in death but was continually acknowledged as a true partner and dear friend with whom this work was done. A popular retelling of their collaborations is published in *The Undoing Project: A Friendship that Changed the World* (2016) by Michael Lewis.

Anyway, in Kahneman and Tversky's various studies (several of which are compiled in Kahneman et al. (1982) although there are many and numerous other collaborators for each over the years), what I above had called "tricks" were better described as heuristics and biases when making judgments given uncertainty. These include availability and representativeness heuristics by which instances and examples that come to mind first push us to specific judgments. Hearing about plane crashes in the news, even if they are to be expected at a certain low (but still unfortunate) frequency, can lead people to be more prone to think they are more likely to be in a plane crash. Watching a basketball player who is on a scoring streak makes us think they have a hot hand and should keep getting the ball and taking shots even though their performance may average out in the long run. As heuristics, these have uses, but they do not work in all situations. We do not always have time to pause and be deliberative when making decisions that have uncertain outcomes. Relying on these heuristics likely contributed to our survival as a species when there had not been data available (or invented) in the forms we have now. However, these heuristics also seem to make us think that a fair coin that had flipped heads five times in a row is "due" to give tails on the next flip even though the chance is 50/50 if the coin really is fair. The coin has no memory of its past flips nor does it "know" what number flip it is about to do.

Kahneman and Tversky also showed that humans demonstrate other tendencies in our reasoning that suggest some of the logics that are championed in data and statistical work are not our default ones psychologically. Anchoring and adjusting happen when we see the same list of numbers to be multiplied together and will estimate one to yield a higher product because the first number to which we "anchored" our estimation was higher. One illustration is provided below where the same numbers in different sequence could produce this effect.

$1 \times 2 \times 3 \times 4 \times 5 \times 6 \times 7 \times 8$

$8 \times 7 \times 6 \times 5 \times 4 \times 3 \times 2 \times 1$

While this is not a statistics problem in its current form, it is an illustration how initial values or information set the stage for how we process information later. This suggests how we think about the likelihood of an event can follow a pattern of anchoring on initial information and then adjusting as more information is introduced. We could imagine this applying with polls and measurement estimates. Indeed, phenomena like this are quite common in psychology studies, with priming and framing effects.

Also, and to borrow from another Kahneman and Tversky example, if we were told about a woman named Linda, a 31-year-old single and bright philosophy degree holder who had been active in social justice and anti-nuclear demonstrations, and then we were asked if she were more likely to be a bank teller or a feminist bank teller, a large number of us would choose the latter (at least at the time of these research studies) because something in her description matches some part of that profile even though the set of all bank tellers is larger than just those bank tellers who identify as feminists. Kahneman and Tversky have also documented a tendency for people to misjudge the adequacy of sample sizes for making inferences and inferring causality when we can only appropriately assert correlation. This appeared even among psychology researchers (Kahneman & Tversky, 1973).

In terms of data work, we can extrapolate from these studies to predict that when working with data, which involves trying to discern a "signal" in the midst of "noise", we are going to have difficulty. Certain types of outcomes or assumptions get privileged in our interpretations and judgments on the basis of our recent encounters or prior knowledge. Thinking with data often requires us taking the time to shift out of System 1 and into System 2 and question our assumptions, and we need to train ourselves to do that for certain activities—like those in data science.

Confirmation Bias

Confirmation bias is the tendency to be more receptive to information that conforms to our expectations or beliefs (Wason, 1960). One of the earliest tests of this was a game where research participants were offered a sequence of numbers—such as 2, 4, 6—by an experimenter who had a specific rule for numbers to follow. This was followed by participants offering their own sequence of three numbers and then being told by the experimenter whether or not that sequence conformed to the rule. Some participants would proceed to guess something like 6, 8, 10 and then 14, 16, 18 before confidently declaring that the rule was to increment each number by 2 when the experimenter's rule was that each number must be greater than the last (thus making 7, 34, 208 also correct). In this case, confirmation of an initial guess was supported and thus the participant stuck with that rather than examining cases that could violate their rule.

Sometimes, we call this tendency "motivated reasoning" (Kunda, 1990), especially when emotion or goals are involved. We like to have our ideas validated and affirmed. If as an educational researcher, I have a specific hope that a new learning intervention increases performance on some assessment and I see signs that it does, I have to make myself really pause and scrutinize the analysis and findings to make sure I am not just seeing what I want to see because I got my desired outcome. It often feels good to be right, and it can feel embarrassing or bad to be wrong. Emotion affects how we see things

(Zadra & Clore, 2011), including how we participate in debates and discussions that involve data.

The presence of confirmation bias and forms of motivated reasoning suggests our default approach with data is not necessarily to simply see and accept what data say. If in a school data analysis activity, students are already favorable to a certain result, changing their minds or getting them to see things otherwise takes more work than just showing them the data. Indeed, we can easily recognize this happening in many facets of daily life when we hear about poll numbers for favored politicians or performance on stocks or in talking about the records for our favorite sports teams. Work needs to be done to create receptivity to other ways of thinking about data and arguments that are supported by data. While there are a range of strategies for getting people to shift their initial judgments based on data, especially when they feel something of importance is at stake, I have found in some classroom research with my colleague Leema Berland that acknowledging what others think and see in data even if you think it is incorrect can be a way to get students to be open to considering other ways of seeing data (Berland & Lee, 2012).

Some educational psychology research has suggested tendencies toward motivated reasoning and confirmation bias contribute to the maintenance of "misconceptions" and science denial (Shtulman, 2017; Sinatra & Hofer, 2021). Relatedly, in some developmental psychology studies, Kuhn (1989) has suggested children struggle to reconcile what evidence says with their prior ideas. If given discrepant evidence, middle school-aged children would exhibit tendencies to discount what the evidence (e.g., data) said if it differed from their prior ideas. Seeing data that are counter to their beliefs or claims can be immediately followed by ignoring or dismissing the data. Some students would even selectively identify portions of available evidence that were supportive of their initial ideas. Indeed, a number of ways for students to respond to data that does not conform to their prior beliefs have been documented—including dismissal and including updating their thinking in light of new evidence that challenges prior knowledge (Chinn & Brewer, 1993). For many current researchers and designers of science education, the goal is often to have data drive changes in prior understandings or beliefs, and so many are working to develop science curricula that creates space and the need to do that (e.g., Edelson et al., 2021; Krajcik & Shin, 2014). Ultimately, Kuhn's argument had been a challenge for this work in that it suggested there was a developmental shift among children necessary to reason scientifically given new information, such as data. This could be interpreted by educators as young children being developmentally incapable of doing reasoning driven by data. However, those restrictive developmental interpretations have been challenged both in journal articles (Metz, 1995) and in national reports (Duschl et al., 2007) given a large amount of evidence that with appropriate scaffolding in science class, a wide range of students from different age groups can reconcile data and claims. All of this is to say that we need not assume that, by default, children are not going to be able to think from data. However, appropriate support is needed for students to develop ways of thinking about data.

Visualization Difficulties

Visualization—often in the form of charts and graphs—are key tools for data science. They are valuable parts of exploratory data analysis and novel forms of visualizing data are in and of themselves valued innovations (Tufte, 1983; Tukey, 1977). However, graphs—including those that show data—are another area where existing research has shown that humans often demonstrate poor performance. In education research, for example, there has been extensive work on misreading of graphs that extend so far as a line graph being interpreted as a picture of the thing being referenced or slope and height being intermixed in questions about motion (Bell & Janvier, 1981; Clement, 1989; Leinhardt et al., 1990; McDermott et al., 1987). Other errors may include treating axes that are discrete and categorical (e.g., California, New Jersey) as reflective of continuous qualities (e.g., the further east a state is, the smaller the population) (Zacks & Tversky, 1999). Some hidden features of specific data chart or graph types can also be neglected in interpretations. For example, pie charts reflect the relative composition of a larger whole, but the size of the pie is not usually depicted to show the different size of a whole (e.g., a pie chart showing student preferences of cats vs dogs in their class shown next to an identically sized pie chart depicting student preferences of cats vs dogs in the entire school have different numbers of students as the base).

Also, while they may be common knowledge in data science, there are data representations that are not widely familiar to all. I recall in one job I had where students worked on a computer-based curriculum that there were many occasions when box and whisker plots were presented for students to interpret. Many times, neither the students nor the other adults in the room had familiarity with this visualization as they had not been exposed to it previously. Histograms are a way of showing density in "bins", and they are not necessarily known nor understood by all. In conversations with many people who have lots of educational experience, I have often had to define histograms because they were unfamiliar.

There are also other types of data visualizations that can invite inaccurate inferences. For example, when the United States has presidential elections, a map of the country with states colored blue or red is used to show which states (and their voting delegates) have been won by which candidate. In several elections, the total land area filled with one color is much more substantial than the other (more red midwestern states, which tend to be quite large, and more blue New England states, which are much smaller). Some take from this the impression that while more delegates may have gone to a candidate who won in geographically smaller states by area, the candidate associated with the larger states (by area) actually had more support. This is because population density and number of people are not represented in these kinds of map data visualizations.

Background knowledge about things that a graph refers to is shown to affect how people interpret the graph. For instance, Shah and Hoeffner (2002) have documented that when (undergraduate) students believe they know more about the subject being referenced in a graph—such as a relationship between the number of car accidents and number of drunk drivers)—they are more likely to state and visually recognize general trends than when the relationship is unknown (e.g., ice cream sales and relative fat content).

Infographics are a genre of information display that typically creatively depicts data in creative ways intermixed with text. For example, an infographic may depict popularity of pizza toppings on a giant image of a pizza with the size of the topping in the picture being proportional to its popularity, blending iconic/pictoral images with quantitative information. Polman and Gebre (2015) have examined infographic interpretation strategies, and information that must be considered in interpreting those include the audience and purpose of the infographic, data sources, and what conventions are being deployed.

One distinction that has been offered for talking about the work of graph interpretation has been provided by Curcio (1987). In order to comprehend what a graph is showing, an interpreter must, at the most elementary level, be able to "read the data". This would involve, for instance, reading out specific values such as in a graph of a specific child's (Stuart) height each year in their first ten years of life (Figure 3.1), reporting the height at year 7. More advanced is "reading between the data", meaning having the ability to combine or distinguish multiple values in the graph. Returning to the height example, reading between the data could ask between which two years did Stuart's height increase the most. Finally, there is "Reading beyond the data", which involves extrapolation or making inferences that take the information from the graph into consideration and then forming a judgment. For example, being asked to estimate what the child's height may be at age 11 or 12 would involve reading beyond the data, as the graph only included heights until age 10.

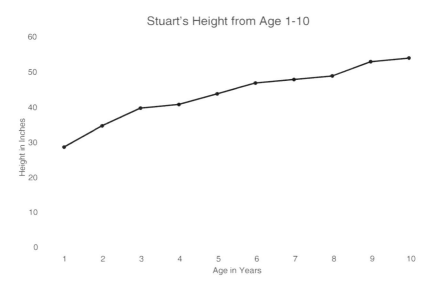

Figure 3.1 A height graph of a hypothetical youth named Stuart.

Some argue that difficulty with graphs is overly emphasized and, under certain circumstances, children can be quite good at understanding graphs. One situation is when the quantities being represented in graphs are dynamically generated, such as with probeware sensors that continuously plot the values as the child is using the tools so they can see what changes under different conditions (Struck & Yerrick, 2010; Zucker et al., 2008). Another is to invite students to create and critique graphs, enabling them to reflect on what is being shown and what are effective ways to show that information (diSessa, 2004; diSessa et al., 1991).

Understanding What Data Are and Why We Care

Having commented on largely some of the known difficulties that people have when reasoning from data I now turn more intentionally to the questions: what does educational research say about what young people think of as data? What do they think data are and how one should be using them? In many respects, this is a moving target. Long ago, data may have been thought of as something related to scientists. In other years, data may have been thought of as something related to computer scientists because they worked with and had courses about data structures. For some, data might have been the name of a popular Star Trek character or it might refer to the unlimited part of their mobile phone service plans. What is summarized here is likely to change with the times, but we do have some prior research investigating young people's conceptions of data.

What Is the Nature of Data and Does Privacy Matter?

I will begin with the observation that while there are a number of concerns voiced about youth and data safety, there needs to be more research on what youth think data are and how they feel about it. Arguably, adults have complex and perhaps even contradictory feelings about data. However, I summarize a few of the studies that have foregrounded students' understandings of the nature of data as it exists and is used in the world as a focal topic.

Leanne Bowler and colleagues (2017) conducted an interview study with teens aged 11–18 in urban public libraries to document what they thought data were. They found two modes of thinking about data. Half associated data as being quantitative information that served as a form of evidence that was tied to science or scientific inquiry. Teens mentioned charts, spreadsheets, tables, and graphs as being centrally associated with data. Science fair was specifically referenced as being an important place where data were important and used, often resulting in more favorable assessments of their science fair projects.

A different set of young people, constituting about a third of the sample, thought of data as tied to digital information. To use a quote from one of Bowler et al.'s participants, data is "stuff that has been created and it's sent across [the internet] and everyone links to it, pretty much" and being like the memory on a mobile device (p. 31). Teens in this study pictured data as being files or storage systems, or even as the green lines of code that moved across the screen in the 1999 science fiction film *The Matrix*. Data about their own digital activities was less familiar, and few expressed concern about the data that were produced and retained from their digital interactions. Youth in this sample were not fully aware of the commercialization of these data nor did they express much concern about these data being collected and used as threats to privacy. To take another youth quote from the study regarding privacy and digital data,

Like, I believe that the invasion of privacy is not such a big deal as long as you don't take severe action and like, the stuff that you say and do and if it's collected in data that you can present... You shouldn't be different things for different people, you know?

(p. 33)

More recently, work by Agesilaou and Kyza (2022) has provided supportive evidence of these tendencies. Their study took place in Cyprus and focused on young students' thinking about matters of data ownership and privacy. The focal age group for them was fifth- and sixth-grade students. In their study with 63 students, there was a tendency among the participants to view data that they obtained from activity trackers as something that they owned and were not really aware of it being shared ownership with a third party (e.g., the company that produces the devices or stores the data in the cloud). Students did not have robust understandings of the technical infrastructure involved. Under different circumstances, they had differing feelings about sharing their data, with different feelings about what the data were about. For example, young people did not seem concerned with sharing their height as data but were more uncomfortable with sharing their city of residence or locations.

These studies are surprisingly among very few that have asked how young people recognize or feel about data. We see there are some germs of understanding and concern like those that have been raised by others who have interrogated the ways in which big data are used in potentially harmful ways (e.g., Philip et al., 2013), but the evidence suggests young people who are not avid privacy advocates have very different views of how data operate in their lives and what might be the concerns and perceived privacy risks about data. Indeed, in my team's own research interviews with high school students, the collection of personal data in digital systems is not seen as concerning and would even be a fair exchange given the customization that results from it (Lee et al., 2022).

How Do Young People Currently Understand What They See in Data?

In statistics education, one established set of labels for how students see data has been published in Konold et al. (2015). In their study, Konold and colleagues worked with a range of interviews across ages and published information sources to find groupings for how students see or view data. They refer to these as "lenses". To illustrate with the support of an example, for the following sections, let's imagine some activity had been run in a middle school classroom—such as how many steps it took for the students in one class to walk from one end of a school playground field to the other. Steps are not really standardized units, which makes it especially amenable to showing variability in a data plot. Figure 3.2 comes from an earlier project of mine and was actual student-generated data for this task (that study is described in Lee et al. (2016)).

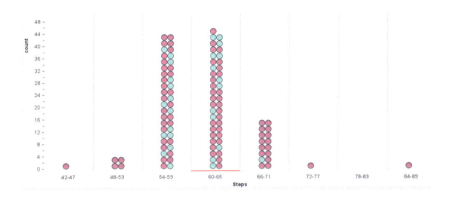

Figure 3.2 A binned plot of the number of steps taken by students as they walked across the field near their playground.

Four Lenses on Data

Data as Pointer

The "data as pointer" lens on data involves seeing data as referring to a particular event or activity from which the data had been generated. In the example of the playground field walk, it would involve statements like "That was when we counted our steps on the field" or "We walked from the monkey bars to the fence". These statements make reference to what the data were about or what had been done to get the data but do not provide any insight into quantities or features of data beyond the setting from which they came. In Konold et al.'s (2015) study, this appeared among younger students, such as those from kindergarten classes. This is not to say that this sort of way of seeing data is underdeveloped or lacking in sophistication—knowing to what data refer and how they came to be can be critically important. Indeed, many of us make such interpretations of data visualizations in this way. For example, there is the famed public health visualization by Jon Snow of the cholera outbreak and Broad Street in London that showed a concentration of illness around a shared water pump on a map. While this can be itself a fascinating source of data inspection, recognizing what this visualization is—the cholera map—can be important and useful.

Data as Case Value

"Data as Case Value" is a lens on data that privileges a single data point and the values of some of its attributes. For instance, in our playground walk example, calling out a specific value—such as the highest one or one associated with a specific person—would be a view on data as case value. This has its uses, to be sure. Looking at a datum is common to get a better sense of a case whether it is of an event or object. Indeed, I will often look at case values when the data come from me and are pooled together from many other people, such as which vote I had cast in an election or where my response resides on a scale for a survey that is taken by many people. On a lot of instructional activities related to graphs and visualizations, a standard exercise is to report out the value of what might be a single data record or chart—or in Curcio's terms, "read the data". What is the growth rate of data scientists according to the Bureau of Labor Statistics (see Figure 1.1)? This is an assessment of being able to extract a bit of that kind of information.

   Again, this is not a bad lens on data, but, if overused or used exclusively when other ways of looking at data are more suited to the question at hand, this can be a problem. When working with students, there is often a focus on extreme values or who is linked to a specific value. Say we return to the steps across the field scenario of Figure 3.2. When this is presented in class, the student who took the most steps of everyone in the class (in this case, between 84 and 89 steps) is often identified and talked about (see Lee (2020) for a play-by-play example). That can end up being the one thing that they remember about a set of data. And it can be understandable why this often gets privileged. In many life and public events—such as athletics—we care about the fastest time ever recorded and standout moments. That is the basis upon which we give awards and recognition. When the value of a financial investment hits a new high, we also care. However, this way of viewing data can be called into question if we were to debate who was the greatest of all time (GOAT) in a given sport or what is the most sound long-term financial investment for growth. We can easily imagine situations where there are the equivalent of one-hit wonders, and while they may hold a single record of note, they did not exhibit a consistent overall tendency to perform in that way. When we look at data for tendency, we begin looking at data as aggregate, described in more detail a couple of sections further below.

Data as Classifier

To look at data as a classifier is to move beyond the focus on a specific value of a given attribute and instead begin to consider multiple instances of datum—cases or points—that share something in common but do comprise the whole collection of data. Returning to our playground field walking example, this could be a categorization of "the taller kids" and "the shorter kids", or if the activity were done across students across multiple class periods, then the period number (students from period 1 and the students from period 2) could be a classifier. Many times in data work, we care about classifications as that helps us to establish different conditions or possible predictors. In data science, cluster analysis and profile analysis help us to create classifications. And training classifiers—such as those used for image or word recognition—is big business in data science.

Viewing data as a classifier invites recognition of certain features of the group, such as absolute or relative frequency for each category. Students might observe that there are only 4 students who are in the categorization of "the taller kids" or 30 students in period two but 26 in period one. Frequency for different categories is useful for looking at values in bar charts and histograms. Naming the classification is also useful and what one might do when looking at the product of a cluster analysis or ways of segmenting data.

Data as Aggregate

Data as aggregate tends to require more work to help students to learn, and in Konold's study, tended to appear more with older students. Seeing data as aggregate involves recognizing tendencies and patterns in the data. Knowing central tendency—such as where seems to be the average even though the data may be spread out or distributed—is one example. Knowing also how data are spread out or if there are concentrations of data is also useful for an aggregate lens. For example, if we consider the bell curve distribution, we expect there to be more concentration of data toward the middle, which, in an ideal situation, would be the mean, median, and the mode. There would be tails as well that shrink as values deviate further from the center.

Speaking about data as aggregate can qualitatively sound like talking about where large amounts of data tend to be or how the distribution is shaped (such as skewed). This means expecting variability to be there in the larger set of data but, regardless of that, expecting there to still be a sort of discernible tendency. Konold and Pollatsek (2002) have referred to this process as a search for a "signal" in "noisy processes", and being able to gain information in light of there being "noise" tends to privilege more data over less as that will help us to better discern the signal. Scientific research that looks at measurements across different conditions—such as those individuals who use one cholesterol drug vs another—relies on this because there is an expectation that the different conditions will tend to yield different results, but the exact values will vary for reasons beyond those that are the focus of the study. Some participants in this hypothetical cholesterol study may consume a lot of foods that tend to increase cholesterol levels and others may not. Everyone's genetic makeup differs as well. However, if one cholesterol drug is more effective than the other, we would expect to see differences in the aggregate, such as a different central tendency.

Getting students to a point where they can comfortably and appropriately see data as aggregate at the right times is a goal of many elementary, middle-grade, and even some high school learning experiences. It sometimes goes by different names, such as local-global (Ben-Zvi & Arcavi, 2001), but the academic literature includes detailed case studies of when students in various learning situations were making this shift and what facilitated it. Often this involves students starting with data as case value and then easing into data as aggregate. However, as Ben-Zvi observes, we want students to be able to move between these ways of seeing data. Sometimes we should focus on individual data points and others we want to look at the aggregate, and in some manner we want to know how those relate to each other such as with outlier sensitivity.

As suggested throughout this overview of the four "lenses" on data documented by Konold et al., my point is to not discount the usefulness of these lenses. This is not strictly a progression from simple to more sophisticated, especially as Ben-Zvi and Arcavi observe the importance of being able to move back and forth. However, it is possible to treat these instructionally in ways that reflect a progression. For example, a classroom teaching experiment about data from case values to aggregate is illustrated in Cobb (1999). In that, he shows how bespoke computer tools that show data values can be used to transform a plot of case values could then be adapted to support learning. Through a detailed analysis, Cobb shows how case values are turned into dotplots whereby density of cases was more apparent, and then over the course of instruction, the class proceeds from those depictions of density data to thinking about groups and aggregate tendencies reflected in the data.

Important Statistical Ideas for Students to Learn

In both longstanding and current research from statistics and data science education, some recommendations for important big ideas about data are surfacing and are being recommended. These represent a different emphasis than discrete skills like being able to read a pictograph and calculate standard deviation. Therefore, these do inch toward a content emphasis, although for them to be useful they all are realized through processes and ways of thinking about data around them and are not bound to a specific technique or named method. Elements of these can be made accessible to a range of grade levels and be treated in more simplified and advanced ways. What I can include here is an introduction to a number of ideas that have been repeatedly named as important over hyper-specific data-science-as-content, and for more research and synthesis on some of these, an excellent summary of big ideas related to reasoning about data is in Biehler et al. (2018).

Measurement

The decision to characterize something through measurement—such as its length in centimeters or weight in kilograms—is an important idea in data science. Often, we treat measures as self-evident or sufficient by themselves for whatever it is we are truly interested in understanding. For instance, a student's grade point average (GPA) is often treated as a statement of "how smart someone is" when it is truly a report of earned (or given) grades from classes as determined by various teachers and their grading systems. It is important, but often challenging, for students to take the time to revisit what is being referenced and appreciate that the measure is (1) constructed and (2) a proxy for something else of interest. This is separate from knowing specifics of how to measure things, like with a ruler or scale (or how GPA is calculated). It is also more than understanding if a selected measure is best represented as a variable that is ordinal, categorical, discrete, continuous, or a ratio—although those do have important implications for what kinds of operations one might use on those measurements. An important way of thinking about this is in recognizing that a measurement represents a decision and sometimes agreement, but could be done in other ways. Returning to the "smart" example, one might opt to look at IQ, standardized test scores, ratings from peers, how many witty comments they make in an hour around peers, number of degrees held, or some combination. These can all have interesting measurement properties—such as having different amounts of noise and precision. But they all have relative strengths and weaknesses. More will be said about the importance of measurement in variability and distribution below.

Variability

Variability across multiple measurements is expected. Indeed, it is core to statistical work because there are assumptions of "noise" in our measurements, but it is also where there may be more predictable, non-random differences. In these two cases, the reason for the variability can differ. One distinction of use comes from Lehrer and Schauble (2007)—the kind that is natural variability and the kind that is measurement variability.

If students are measuring the height of plants, it will be the true that some plants will grow taller than other plants. That is natural variability. If we had perfect measurements, we would see this. However, measurement can produce variability too for a number of other reasons. Some instruments simply do not provide the same precision. A ruler that is broken only into centimeters may not have markings that go down to millimeters. Also, some instruments create more risks for measurement variability. If we tried to measure adult human height with a single-foot-long ruler, it would be necessary to move the ruler multiple times, which creates the added challenge of keeping the rule sliding up or down the same amount each time it is moved. There is error which can come from sliding the ruler in ways that are inconsistent (Lehrer et al., 2007). Also, while we develop procedures in scientific research to reach reliability, there can be subtle differences that people see differently for a variety of reasons.

Measurement variability can be explored by having learners actively participate in measurement, whether it is through the creation of their own measurement instruments or in the use of existing measurement instruments to collect data (Petrosino et al., 2003). The benefit of having learners do this work is that they have experiential resources to draw upon in order to recognize how measurement variability came to be reflected in a set of data. They may recall being distracted or uncertain or recognize that multiple people involved may have used slightly different techniques whether intentional or not. Natural variability can be more challenging and is arguably one of the kinds of variability we try to explain or predict better through scientific and statistical investigation.

Other forms of variability are to be expected by virtue of intentional manipulation. In an experiment, we may intentionally establish specific conditions that differ from one another (e.g., measurements taken in one location and measurements taken in another location) in order to see how the change in one variable (e.g., location) affects the other. Another form of variability is sampling variability and how much we expect samples to differ from one another and the "true" distribution (for nice illustrative examples, see the GAISE report by Franklin et al. (2007)).

Distribution

Distribution encompasses characteristics of a set of related measurements such as shape, center, spread, or density that we often associate with visual depictions but are thought of as emergent qualities of data that come about due to variability. Thinking about data as aggregate is especially important here as these characteristics are used to speak to a property of data rather than to a single case, datum, or point. Given tendencies for learners to talk in terms of individual data points or cases, there are some recognized strategies to help learners become more attuned to distributions such as welcoming and building on informal language such as "clumps" (Konold et al., 2002) where there appear to be a lot of data in a visualization and "bumps" in the overall visualized shape of a distribution that involves many data points. Other approaches include moving from data plots that show individual case values and then how those can be re-seen as frequencies or densities of those cases (such as in the Cobb (1999) example referenced above). It is possible to sequence activities so that there are different ways of making certain qualities salient—such as drawing the overall shape of the distribution, partitioning the distribution into increments such as quartiles, or matching other forms of data representation such as box plots with other data visualizations. For examples, refer to Bakker and Gravemeijer (2004) and Cobb (1999).

In distribution, I would also include measures of center—such as an average. Stating what is the center of a distribution is one way of describing that distribution. However, much of the emphasis in school instruction has been on the algorithms for computing a measure of center—the arithmetic mean, median, or mode—but not as much thoughtful consideration of when and how to use these measures and for what purpose. For example, the mean exhibits more outlier sensitivity than the median, and it is also possible to have a mean or median but the exact value for those may not actually be a point in the data distribution. Watson and Moritz (2000) have documented some of the conceptual challenges associated with students' reasoning about the mean. In their study, more advanced students tended to think of the mean as a balance point in a data set or as a method of "fair share" distribution. Undergraduate students have expressed difficulty with this as well, such as when they are given computational problems that would involve a weighted mean (Pollatsek et al., 1981). For example, computing the GPA for a student who transferred three years of courses at a 3.0 GPA and a 3.8 GPA for two years' worth at another university would not be 3.4 GPA if the number of courses taken per year were consistent, because more time was spent with a 3.0 GPA. Also, there are other measures that can be useful under certain circumstances (such as geometric means).

Inference

Statistical inference involves taking some immediate information, such as a sample of data, and using that to make a determination that extends beyond that sample. Inferential statistics involve the tests (like a t-test) taught in many introductory statistics courses that involve considering the likelihood of null hypotheses being true and how likely the current distribution of data would have come about by chance. That has its complexities familiar to many statistics teachers and students, although it is useful in professional data science as well as is broadly used in quantitative scientific research.

Informal statistical inference does not rely on specific tests that inferential statistics uses and emphasizes intuitions about data and what can be inferred. Makar and Rubin (2018) offer a concise framework for describing informal statistical inference as "a probabilistic generalization made from data". While brief, this captures a lot.

An inference being probabilistic means that there is uncertainty, and that is part and parcel of the inference. While the likelihood may be high, statistical inferences do not involve exhaustive and demonstrative proof in the same way that first order formal logic (e.g. if p, then q) might. For example, if we were taking a measurement of presidential approval rates in the United States by calling 1,000 randomly selected phone numbers, we draw on a sample of the larger population, but we cannot know exactly the level of approval for the entire population at that moment in time. But assuming that we know something about the population from this is what makes this a generalization, as this inference refers to more than the sample. And, finally, the inference is from data and so has some accountability to referring to or basing itself on a set of data. This is different from disregarding the data and inferring some conclusion must be true because it aligns with preferences. For example, someone might infer that organic foods are better genetically modified organisms because they are classified as organic or because an online influencer said so, but those are different from looking at statistical data and basing judgments on that.

Statistical inferences can be used in many ways. We may want to make an inference about the population from a sample—such as in the presidential approval poll example above. We may want to make an inference about whether one condition (experimental drug a) tends to yield different outcomes than another condition (experimental drug b). We may want to make predictions, such as how many points an athlete is likely to score in a game given knowledge of past performance.

A form of informal inference, which can be developed at a young age, can be demonstrated through comparison of two different distributions of data (Watson & Moritz, 1999). Without using formal hypothesis tests, students ranging from third to ninth grade in Watson & Moritz's study had shown the use of multiple strategies—visual (features of a plot) and numerical (specific values or calculations)—to see differences in distributions and support claims. However, it is important to note that there are tendencies to initially focus on individual data points rather than aggregates (local vs global, see Ben-Zvi & Arcavi (2001)). This can be navigated with some careful teacher probing and support to integrate their strategies for distinguishing and comparing two data sets (see Lee & DuMont, 2010, which illustrates students integrating strategies for comparing data sets).

Sampling

Sampling is prominent in probabilistic and statistical reasoning, as many types of inferences are based on samples. How samples are understood can be complex in that students do not necessarily default to recognizing a single sample as one out of many possible outcomes. For example, Shaugnessy and Ciancetta (2002) have examined how middle and high school students can expect a probabilistic outcome to be a certain outcome—if a spinner is expected to land on black 50% of the time and white 50% of the time, but a sample of ten spins yields 60% black and 40% white, many students will think that 50% is wrong even though the 50% split is what should come about from infinite spins. Saldanha and Thompson (2002) observed in another study that some high school students would look to an individual sample as being adequate in representing the larger population. Other high school students in the study were more adept at thinking of a single sample as being one of many possible and that repeated samples would themselves form their own sampling distribution, from which more robust inferences and levels of confidence could be stated. This latter group of students appeared to expect variability to appear across multiple random samples from the same population. This difference was considered of note and reflective of the need to help students further develop their thinking about sampling. There are some ways to help students to explore sample spaces, such as through literally scooping samples out of a large container of marbles or running computer simulations with repeated sampling (Abrahamson, 2009).

In statistics, random sampling is often treated as the ideal. In designing sampling strategies, students can also be enticed to privilege some heuristics in sample construction over favoring randomness. Schwartz et al. (1998) documented how elementary students are able to opt for a random sample to make inferences in some contexts, but then favor non-random approaches in others. For example, when asked to devise a sampling approach for determining the mix of different colored marbles in an urn or to figure out the gender composition of their school, students would often opt for a random sampling. However, when asked to devise a sampling strategy for students' interest in a school fair, students would opt for strategies such as purposefully selecting a certain number of students from each grade or defining types of students and making sure that all types were intentionally selected for sampling. The context of the situation affected what students considered appropriate strategies to make inferences that would sometimes conform to what is desirable statistically and sometimes not.

Association

Finding relationships between variables—such as changes in bivariate data plotted on *X-Y* axes—can be a goal in data analysis. However, distinguishing between correlation and causation is important and requires careful consideration that is based on prior knowledge of what is being referenced. That is, one must understand that it would make little sense to believe that the number of films that actor Nicholas Cage appears in causes an increase in drowning deaths in swimming pools (Goldman, 2014). There may be a (spurious) correlation, but it is not a causal relationship.

In general, understanding and maintaining consistency in reasoning across multiple variables can be challenging. For example, learning to control variables and examine the effects of single variables when all other factors are removed from consideration is a strategy for working with data and conducting experiments that often requires teaching (Chen & Klahr, 1999; Kuhn, 2010). Also, keeping the effects of a variable consistent in thinking through multivariable situations can be a challenge. In studies of fourth graders, for example, Kuhn (2007) found that after training where students demonstrated accurate understanding of the effects from individual independent variables on a dependent variable, those same students' reasoning about a depdendent variable when multiple independent variables were involved became inconsistent. To illustrate what that looks like, here is a hypothetical situation: imagine children were given data on a beverage stand's sales and through investigation of individual variables, they found that outdoor temperature was positively associated with more sales, the presence of an outdoor public event like a concert or fair was also associated with higher sales, and who was working at the beverage stand did not have an association. On a later task when asked to consider multiple variables, some students would look at a situation with warm weather and an outdoor event and predict sales would be lower, or that sales with a specific employee during cold weather on a day with no public events would be high despite employee staffing not having an effect, and cold weather and the lack of a public event should have a negative effect. While a child could produce sensible-sounding justifications for why they make these predictions (e.g., the employee is more motivated to move around more and push for more sales to keep themselves warm and give people something to do since there isn't anything else nearby to keep customers entertained?), the tendency is not to rely on the data given or the reasoning around variable associations previously determined in the activity.

Difficulty with multivariate thinking appears across ages (Kuhn & Dean, 2004). This is not to say that multivariate thinking is not attainable—people do already develop scientific multivariate competencies if they do not already demonstrate them in some other non-experimental contexts. While we may want to intentionally teach students to engage in multivariate reasoning in certain "scientific" ways, it is also worth acknowledging that there can be good reasons why what may be classified as incorrect multivariate thinking is a good thing. For example, variables can mediate or interact with one another, leading to unexpected outcomes.

Still-Looming Questions Regarding How Humans Think about Data

The above are areas that have decent-sized histories of prior research. There are, of course, more questions that need to be asked for each of those and revisiting assumptions that should be done regularly. For data science—extending in both process and content considerations—there are some topics that need more study with respect to how people think about these things or approach them, as we expect at least in the near term they will be important.

One is the intersection of computational thinking and data work. Computational thinking is a term that has been in the literature for a while but ascended rapidly following Jeannette Wing's (2006) discussion of the broad usefulness of using the same ways of thinking about challenges in the way that is encouraged given the tools of computation, often but not exclusively, programming. If we take programming as one robust area of computational thinking, acknowledging that it is not the sole space nor purpose for it, there is an unanswered question about how understanding programming and understanding data are supportive of one another and how they may create challenges. In the long run, must someone learn to program and be adept at it in order to do the work of data science? And does that hold true as we increasingly create tools and supports that can help with code generation or reduce the thinking demands that code creation and editing often take? There are different types of programming languages and programming environments—do those make a difference?

Another is probabilistic and Bayesian reasoning which embraces uncertainty from the start. Much of the way statistics is taught now follows Frequentist approaches, and testing of null hypotheses as a key way to make inferences. There are also simulation approaches and different ways of thinking about uncertainty that are gaining popularity in data science. We need to know more about the learning of these ways of making inferences and predictions, especially given the work we know about difficulties with judgments under uncertainty from Kahneman and Tversky described above. How people learn and understand different machine learning approaches and algorithms will likely be another topic of interest (Shapiro & Fiebrink, 2019), especially with the growth of interest in AI that has been trained using machine learning techniques.

Given the disputes on curriculum, such as in California (see the heterogenous set of perspectives in Boaler et al. (2024)), there are empirical questions about what mathematics experiences and ideas are key to success in data science work and which are less so. As stated earlier, work on how people learn about and think regarding topics of ethics, privacy, and complex social matters in which data science plays a part will need further development. Some work relevant to that will be discussed in Chapter 6. And, of course, there are related questions of access and participation—what are the strategies by which we can make data science available for all? With that in mind, I now turn to an examination of how data science has been taught and represented thus far in schools.

References

Abrahamson, D. (2009). Orchestrating semiotic leaps from tacit to cultural quantitative reasoning—The case of anticipating experimental outcomes of a quasi-binomial random generator. *Cognition and Instruction, 27*(3), 175–224.

Agesilaou, A., & Kyza, E. A. (2022). Whose data are they? Elementary school students' conceptualization of data ownership and privacy of personal digital data. *International Journal of Child-Computer Interaction, 33*, 100462. https://doi.org/10.1016/j.ijcci.2022.100462

Bakker, A., & Gravemeijer, K. P. (2004). Learning to reason about distribution. In D. Ben-Zvi & J. Garfield (Eds.), *The challenge of developing statistical literacy, reasoning and thinking* (pp. 147–168). Dordrecht: Springer.

Batz, J. M. (2021). "Nik" — The zero in vigesimal Maya mathematics. *Bulletin of the AAS, 53*(1). https://baas.aas.org/pub/2021n1i336p03

Bell, A., & Janvier, C. (1981). The interpretation of graphs representing situations. *For the Learning of Mathematics, 2*(1), 34–42. Retrieved from https://www.jstor.org/stable/40240746

Ben-Zvi, D., & Arcavi, A. (2001). Junior high school students' construction of global views of data and data representations. *Educational Studies in Mathematics, 45*(1), 35–65. https://doi.org/10.1023/A:1013809201228

Berland, L. K., & Lee, V. R. (2012). In pursuit of consensus: Disagreement and legitimization during small group argumentation. *International Journal of Science Education, 34*(12), 1857–1882. https://doi.org/10.1080/09500693.2011.645086

Biehler, R., Frischemeier, D., Reading, C., & Shaughnessy, J. M. (2018). Reasoning about data. In D. Ben-Zvi, K. Makar, & J. Garfield (Eds.), *International handbook of research in statistics education* (pp. 139–192). Cham: Springer International Publishing.

Boaler, J., Conrad, B., Ford, B., Mazzeo, R., & Nelson, J. (2024). Three views on the California math framework. *Notices of the American Mathematical Society, 71*(6), 797–805. https://doi.org/10.1090/noti2957

Bowler, L., Acker, A., Jeng, W., & Chi, Y. (2017). "It lives all around us": Aspects of data literacy in teen's lives. *Proceedings of the Association for Information Science and Technology, 54*(1), 27–35. https://doi.org/10.1002/pra2.2017.14505401004

Chen, Z., & Klahr, D. (1999). All other things being equal: Acquisition and transfer of the control of variables strategy. *Child Development, 70*(5), 1098–1120. doi:https://doi.org/10.1111/1467-8624.00081

Chinn, C. A., & Brewer, W. F. (1993). The role of anomalous data in knowledge acquisition: A theoretical framework and implications for science instruction. *Review of Educational Research, 63*(1), 1–49.

Clement, J. (1989). The concept of variation and misconceptions in Cartesian graphing. *Focus on Learning Problems in Mathematics, 11*(1–2), 77–87.

Cobb, P. (1999). Individual and collective mathematical development: The case of statistical data analysis. *Mathematical Thinking and Learning, 1*(1), 5–43. https://doi.org/10.1207/s15327833mtl0101_1

Curcio, F. R. (1987). Comprehension of mathematical relationships expressed in graphs. *Journal for Research in Mathematics Education JRME, 18*(5), 382–393. doi:10.5951/jresematheduc.18.5.0382

diSessa, A. A. (2004). Metarepresentation: Native competence and targets for instruction. *Cognition and Instruction, 22*(3), 293–331.

diSessa, A. A., Hammer, D., Sherin, B., & Kolpakowski, T. (1991). Inventing graphing: Meta-representational expertise in children. *Journal of Mathematical Behavior, 10*, 117–160.

Duschl, R. A., Schweingruber, H. A., & Shouse, A. W. (2007). *Taking science to school: Learning and teaching science in grades K-8*. Washington, DC: The National Academies Press.

Edelson, D. C., Reiser, B. J., McNeill, K. L., Mohan, A., Novak, M., Mohan, L., … Deutch Noll, J. (2021). Developing research-based instructional materials to support large-scale transformation of science teaching and learning: The approach of the OpenSciEd middle school program. *Journal of Science Teacher Education, 32*(7), 780–804.

Feigenson, L., Dehaene, S., & Spelke, E. (2004). Core systems of number. *Trends in Cognitive Sciences, 8*(7), 307–314. https://doi.org/10.1016/j.tics.2004.05.002

Franklin, C., Kader, G., Mewborn, D., Moreno, J., Peck, R., Perry, M., & Scheaffer, R. (2007). *Guidelines for assessment and instruction in statistics education (GAISE) report: A pre-k–12 curriculum framework*. Alexandria, VA: American Statistical Association.

Goldman, A. (2014). Deaths by swimming pool drowning vs. Nicholas cage films and other spurious correlations. Retrieved from https://www.wnycstudios.org/podcasts/otm/articles/spurious-correlations

Kahneman, D. (2011). *Thinking, fast and slow*. New York, NY: Farrar, Strauss, and Giroux.

Kahneman, D., Slovic, P., & Tversky, A. (1982). *Judgment under uncertainty: Heuristics and biases*. Cambridge University Press.

Kahneman, D., & Tversky, A. (1973). On the psychology of prediction. *Psychological Review, 80*(4), 237–251. https://doi.org/10.1037/h0034747

Konold, C., Higgins, T., Russell, S. J., & Khalil, K. (2015). Data seen through different lenses. *Educational Studies in Mathematics, 88*(3), 305–325. https://doi.org/10.1007/s10649-013-9529-8

Konold, C., & Pollatsek, A. (2002). Data analysis as the search for signals in noisy processes. *Journal for Research in Mathematics Education, 33*(4), 259–289.

Konold, C., Robinson, A., Khalil, K., Pollatsek, A., Well, A. D., Wing, R., & Mayr, S. (2002). Students' use of modal clumps to summarize data. Paper presented at the Sixth International Conference on Teaching Statistics, Cape Town, South Africa.

Krajcik, J., & Shin, N. (2014). Project-based learning. In R. K. Sawyer (Ed.), *The Cambridge handbook of the learning sciences* (pp. 275–297). Cambridge: Cambridge University Press.

Kuhn, D. (1989). Children and adults as intuitive scientists. *Psychological Review, 96*(4), 674–689.

Kuhn, D. (2007). Reasoning about multiple variables: Control of variables is not the only challenge. *Science Education, 91*(5), 710–726. https://doi.org/10.1002/sce.20214

Kuhn, D. (2010). What is scientific thinking and how does it develop? In U. Goswami (Ed.), *The Wiley-Blackwell handbook of childhood cognitive development* (pp. 497–523). West Sussex: Blackwell Publishers.

Kuhn, D., & Dean Jr, D. (2004). Connecting scientific reasoning and causal inference. *Journal of Cognition and Development, 5*(2), 261–288. https://doi.org/10.1207/s15327647jcd0502_5

Kunda, Z. (1990). The case for motivated reasoning. *Psychological Bulletin, 108*(3), 480–498. https://doi.org/10.1037/0033-2909.108.3.480

Lee, V. R. (2020). Supporting complex multimodal expression around representations of data: Experience matters. In P. Sengupta, B. Kim, & M.-C. Shanahan (Eds.), *Critical, transdisciplinary and embodied approaches in STEM education* (pp. 217–231). Chalm: Springer.

Lee, V. R., Delaney, V., & Sarin, P. (2022). Eliciting high school students' conceptions and intuitions about algorithmic bias. In J. Vahrenhold, K. Fisler, M. Hauswirth, & D. Franklin (Eds.), *Proceedings of the 2022 ACM Conference on International Computing Education Research V.2* (pp. 35–36). Lugani and Virtual Event, Switzerland: ACM.

Lee, V. R., Drake, J. R., & Thayne, J. L. (2016). Appropriating quantified self technologies to improve elementary statistical teaching and learning. *IEEE Transactions on Learning Technologies, 9*(4), 354–365. https://doi.org/10.1109/TLT.2016.2597142

Lee, V. R., & DuMont, M. (2010). An exploration into how physical activity data-recording devices could be used in computer-supported data investigations. *International Journal of Computers for Mathematical Learning, 15*(3), 167–189. https://doi.org/10.1007/s10758-010-9172-8

Lehrer, R., Kim, M.-j., & Schauble, L. (2007). Supporting the development of conceptions of statistics by engaging students in measuring and modeling variability. *International Journal of Computers for Mathematical Learning, 12*, 195–216.

Lehrer, R., & Schauble, L. (2007). Contrasting emerging conceptions of distribution in contexts of error and natural variation. In M. Lovett & P. Shah (Eds.), *Thinking with data* (pp. 149–176). Mahwah, NJ: Lawrence Erlbaum.

Leinhardt, G., Zaslavsky, O., & Stein, M. M. (1990). Functions, graphs, and graphing: Tasks, learning, and teaching. *Review of Educational Research, 60*, 1–64.

Lewis, M. (2016). *The undoing project: A friendship that changed the world*. New York: W. W. Norton.

Makar, K., & Rubin, A. (2018). Learning about statistical inference. In D. Ben-Zvi, K. Makar, & J. Garfield (Eds.), *International handbook of research in statistics education* (pp. 261–294). Cham: Springer International Publishing.

McDermott, L. C., Rosenquist, M. L., & van Zee, E. (1987). Student difficulties in connecting graphs and physics: Examples from kinematics. *American Journal of Physics, 55*(6), 505–513.

Metz, K. E. (1995). Reassessment of developmental constraints on children's science instruction. *Review of Educational Research, 65*(2), 93–127.

Petrosino, A., Lehrer, R., & Schauble, L. (2003). Structuring error and experimental variation as distribution in the fourth grade. *Mathematical Thinking and Learning, 5*(2&3), 131–156.

Philip, T. M., Schuler-Brown, S., & Way, W. (2013). A framework for learning about big data with mobile technologies for democratic participation: Possibilities, limitations, and unanticipated obstacles. *Technology, Knowledge and Learning, 18*(3), 103–120. https://doi.org/10.1007/s10758-013-9202-4

Pollatsek, A., Lima, S., & Well, A. D. (1981). Concept or computation: Students' understanding of the mean. *Educational Studies in Mathematics, 12*(2), 191–204.

Polman, J. L., & Gebre, E. H. (2015). Towards critical appraisal of infographics as scientific inscriptions. *Journal of Research in Science Teaching, 52*(6), 868–893. https://doi.org/10.1002/tea.21225

Saldanha, L., & Thompson, P. (2002). Conceptions of sample and their relationship to statistical inference. *Educational Studies in Mathematics, 51*, 257–270.

Saxe, G. B. (1991). *Culture and cognitive development: Studies in mathematical understanding.* Hillsdale, NJ: Erlbaum.

Schwartz, D. L., Goldman, S. R., Vye, N. J., & Barron, B. J. (1998). Aligning everyday and mathematical reasoning: The case of sampling assumptions. In S. P. Lajoie (Ed.), *Reflections on statistics: Learning, teaching, and assessment in grades K-12* (pp. 233–273). New York, NY: Routledge.

Seife, C. (2000). *Zero: The biography of a dangerous idea.* New York: Penguin.

Shah, P., & Hoeffner, J. (2002). Review of graph comprehension research: Implications for instruction. *Educational Psychology Review, 14*(1), 47–69. https://doi.org/10.1023/A:1013180410169

Shapiro, R. B., & Fiebrink, R. (2019). Introduction to the special section: Launching an agenda for research on learning machine learning. *ACM Transactions on Computing Education, 19*(4), Article 30. https://doi.org/10.1145/3354136

Shaughnessy, J., & Ciancetta, M. (2002). *Students' understanding of variability in a probability environment.* Paper presented at the Sixth international conference on teaching statistics: Developing a statistically literate society, Cape Town, South Africa.

Shtulman, A. (2017). *Scienceblind: Why our intuitive theories about the world are so often wrong.* New York: Hachette UK.

Sinatra, G. M., & Hofer, B. K. (2021). *Science denial: Why it happens and what to do about it.* New York: Oxford University Press.

Struck, W., & Yerrick, R. (2010). The effect of data acquisition-probeware and digital video analysis on accurate graphical representation of kinetics in a high school physics class. *Journal of Science Education and Technology, 19*(2), 199–211.

Tufte, E. R. (1983). *The visual display of quantitative information.* Cheshire, CT: Graphics Press.

Tukey, J. W. (1977). *Exploratory data analysis.* Reading, MA: Addison-Wesley.

Wason, P. C. (1960). On the failure to eliminate hypotheses in a conceptual task. *Quarterly Journal of Experimental Psychology, 12*(3), 129–140.

Watson, J. M., & Moritz, J. B. (1999). The beginning of statistical inference: Comparing two data sets. *Educational Studies in Mathematics, 37*(2), 145–168. https://doi.org/10.1023/A:1003594832397

Watson, J. M., & Moritz, J. B. (2000). The longitudinal development of understanding of average. *Mathematical Thinking and Learning, 2*(1&2), 11–50.

Wiggins, C., & Jones, M. L. (2023). *How data happened: A history from the age of reason to the age of algorithms*. New York: WW Norton & Company.
Wing, J. M. (2006). Computational thinking. *Communications of the ACM, 49*(3), 33–35.
Zacks, J., & Tversky, B. (1999). Bars and lines: A study of graphic communication. *Memory & Cognition, 27*(6), 1073–1079. https://doi.org/10.3758/BF03201236
Zadra, J. R., & Clore, G. L. (2011). Emotion and perception: The role of affective information. *WIREs Cognitive Science, 2*(6), 676–685. https://doi.org/10.1002/wcs.147
Zucker, A. A., Tinker, R., Staudt, C., Mansfield, A., & Metcalf, S. (2008). Learning science in grades 3–8 using probeware and computers: Findings from the TEEMSS II project. *Journal of Science Education and Technology, 17*(1), 42–48.

Teaching Data Science in Schools

4

Data science education, especially for K-12, is typically thought about in terms of school—and what are the classroom learning experiences that make it up. These experiences are brought about through curriculum materials, lesson resources, technologies, and teachers. There has been work in prior decades before data science education became something we envisioned for K-12. That had tended to be represented in approaches to teaching statistics and data literacy, as the term "data science" was not yet in wide use. In addition to that, there has also been recent and still continues to be interesting new research and development activities involving schools and classrooms that explicitly present themselves as being about and for data science education, now that it is an appreciated and valued term.

This chapter summarizes some of those efforts from the research community, past and present. It is knowingly limited in that new projects and efforts are continually appearing as new ideas are conceived and funded. Also, the technology landscape that has made data science an area of fascination continuously changes to make some things that seemed difficult in the past much easier to do now. For example, bringing complex data visualizations to students had once been a very advanced and ambitious idea for science classrooms (Gomez et al., 1998). Now, we can do quick web searches or scan social media to find any number of visualizations. Similarly, there was a time when teaching computer programming in schools was remarkably ambitious, as we could not even assume that most classrooms had computers (Papert, 1980). However, we now have widespread initiatives like the "Hour of Code" (Yauney et al., 2023) and tangible programming toys built for young

DOI: 10.4324/9781003385264-4

children (Hamilton et al., 2020). However, in education research and design, understanding what has been done before even if things are changing can give us some insight into what things seem to work and why—and can help us to situate different lines of research and development work that is still in the pipeline.

Precedent Approaches

Data is not a new topic for schools, and it has been part of curricula well before the current spike in interest in data science. The topic already exists in some form in standards, although data are not typically made such a prominent focus relative to other topics and ideas. Undoubtedly, there have been motivated teachers and researchers who have pursued data instruction in decades prior that may not have even made it to publication. Rubin (2020) names some from the late 80s and mid-1990s, such as *Used Numbers* (1989) and modules in other curricular series. However, there was certainly one especially notable National Science Foundation effort that made it to print: *Investigations in Number, Data, and Space* produced by TERC, Kent State University, and the University of Buffalo that had been published in the 1990s. As an elementary-level reform math curriculum, data and measurement figured prominently (even in the title). In the lessons from that curriculum, students would be directly involved in activities that involved collecting data and obtaining measurements to examine through investigative processes. A large emphasis was on data representation, communicating with representations of data, and exploratory data analysis. Several developers of the curriculum were also involved in early published academic research studies on student thinking related to data (e.g., Mokros & Russell, 1995).

Lessons in this curriculum emphasized students engaging in issues of measurement, active data collection, data representation, and data analysis. For example, in the grade 5 unit of *Investigations, Data: Kids, Cats, and Ads* (Rubin & Mokros, 1998), students pursue investigations ranging from how long they can stand on one foot to measuring the lengths of cats to determining how much newspaper page space is dedicated to advertisements. Over a series of lessons for each investigation, the class comes to agreement on what are the attributes to record on "data cards" that they make, consider what are some distributional features of various plots, and discuss various samples of known and unknown sources to make inferences. Examples akin to what this unit provided are shown in Figure 4.1. Computer software to support the visualization of data was also provided, based on some earlier work on tools like *Tabletop* (discussed further in the Technology section below).

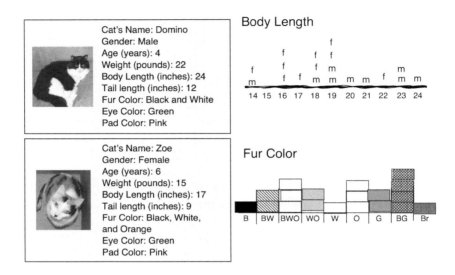

Figure 4.1 Example of cat data cards and data plots as represented in the *Investigations* curriculum.

The What Works Clearinghouse (WWC) initiative of the Institute for Education Sciences (IES) is a unit within the US Department of Education that provides recommendations and reports of curricula. The WWC website contains reports on instructional resources that have been subject to evaluation research and deemed sufficiently evidence-based—such as having specific kinds of experimental designs like randomized controlled trials and outcome measures—for guiding educator practice. Dozens of studies had been identified by IES that analyzed the effectiveness of the *Investigations* curriculum, although in 2013, only two were considered to meet the WWC evidence standards. Given the available information from those studies, *Investigations* "was found to have potentially positive effects on mathematics achievement for elementary school students" (US Department of Education, 2013). It is worth observing that while the other studies did not meet the standards for IES because they used different study designs, they were still rigorously peer-reviewed and pertinent for the research community. Not all research can nor should immediately land on conclusions about effectiveness, despite that being a frequent desire and area of interest and concern from the public.

This curriculum has been updated and is still in use in schools. It has come out in multiple editions, with the third published in 2016, and professional development is still offered by TERC.

Stand-alone Data Science Instruction

High school curriculum to provide data science to students through an explicit branding has also been developed. One example is *Introduction to Data Science (IDS)* (Gould et al., 2018), a stand-alone unit developed at Center X at the University of California, Los Angeles. IDS was created in partnership with Los Angeles Unified School District and was a year-long curriculum that encouraged students to develop their intuitions about data by thinking about variability and distribution as well as measures of center. The R programming environment is used regularly. Students engage in lab activities where they manipulate and visualize data. Through both analog and digital experiences, students explore the nature of their own eating habits or whether female or male characters differ in how frequently they tend to survive in horror movies. *IDS* includes what is called "participatory sensing" campaigns where students are asked to collect data outside of class time so that they can examine a locally or personally relevant topic with real data. Besides the food investigation, others can include water usage in their homes and neighborhoods.

The data cycle—a version of the process that has been identified in Wild and Pfannkuch (1999) and discussed in the *GAISE II* report (Bargagliotti et al., 2020) and discussed in the Data-Science-as-Process section of Chapter 2—is emphasized and explicitly revisited throughout (see Figure 4.2). A key message of this curriculum is that work with data is part of an investigative process involving questions and careful consideration of the data that is available or would be appropriate to analyze in service of answering those questions.

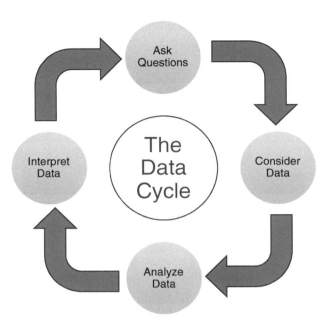

Figure 4.2 IDS's data cycle.

While there is much in *IDS* that echoes statistics statistical topics such as measures of center, sampling, correlation, and common data representations like histograms and scatterplots, there are other intentional efforts to point, as an introduction, toward data science as it is understood today. These include the use of programming environments like *R* and some introductory methods for analyzing data computationally such as clustering, decision trees, and social network analysis. At its core, the message of *IDS* is that data science is about an investigative process, although certain tools and techniques may be seen as more common or foundational toward future data science work.

Other units for secondary grades that integrate some programming have also been developed or are in development. *Bootstrap* (bootstrapworld.org) is an organization that creates computer science-integrated curricular units that are usable from middle school upward. In their own data science unit, they introduce students to computer programming practices of code writing using the language *Pyret*. Currently, with acknowledgment of the debates around the role of Algebra 2 content in the California mathematics curriculum, they are developing a data science unit that integrates Algebra

2. This will include topics such as logarithmic and exponential relationships as well as quadratics. *CourseKata* (see Son et al., 2021) develops what had originally been a digital college statistics curriculum informed by cognitive psychology research that has been expanded for use in high schools with in-unit applets and integration with *R*. The mathematics instruction resource group known as *youcubed* has also developed a stand-alone unit that emphasizes discussion and collaborative interpretation of data (see Boaler et al., in press).

Data Cards and Unplugged Approaches

One stand-alone approach of note is underway in Germany at the University of Paderborn for grades 5–13 and involves both programming notebook-based instruction on data science and also "unplugged" approaches. Unplugged approaches are ones that do not require or expect a computer to be present for the instructional approach, although the content of the lesson and the approach may be in service of developing understandings about computation. Of note has been an analog "data cards" approach that helps students explore and construct decision trees (Podworny et al., 2021). In that activity, cards with information on them (such as nutrition facts) are colored in blue or yellow. The blue cards represent training data and the yellow represent test data. Students take a stack of cards and develop decision rules to classify the foods as ones that are recommended or not for nutritional value and use colored paper clips to "classify" their cards. This progresses to establishing a multileveled tree, with the extension to work in a *Jupyter Notebook*. Along the way, the students examine the challenges and limitations of the data cards and the decision trees that they create in order to develop a critical eye on the algorithms they invent and on decision tree creation in general. More information is available at https://www.prodabi.de/en/.

Integrated Classroom Approaches

For situations where schools opt not to or are unable to offer a dedicated unit or course exclusively on data science, some developers have begun to explore how to combine data science with existing courses that are not from their math departments. However, there are efforts underway to move beyond mathematics classes, as traditionally conceived, and extend into other disciplines. For a number of reasons, including those that reflect on our current understanding how important it is to learn new ideas in the contexts in which they would be used and for what is already a full curriculum, teaching data and data science across the disciplines is being advocated (Jiang et al., 2022). Areas and examples of various disciplines and subject areas that have been explored are listed below.

English Language Arts

Language has been an interesting space for data science work, especially with respect to artificial intelligence. The *StoryQ* project involves integrations with the CODAP (Common Online Data Analysis Platform) platform (see the Technology section below) and helps high school students to "see beneath the hood" of text-based artificial intelligence. For example, working with clickbait headlines and spam, students participate in labeling of data and training a model to do classification (Horton et al., 2023). They detect features from language samples and evaluate models with data visualizations, as well as even broach some sentiment analysis (Chao et al., 2024). This project uses a co-design paradigm with teachers, and early research on teachers' experiences suggests that it is one way for English teachers to feel more comfortable with artificial intelligence topics (Tatar et al., 2024).

Another, based out of Stanford University, is the *ELAlytics* project that integrates data literacy experiences in middle school English Language Arts (ELA) through the use of visualizations of literary texts that students are reading in class in terms of word frequency, sentence length, and even some sentiment analysis. Similar to *StoryQ* and other new curricular design research endeavors, ELAlytics is based on teacher co-design (Lee et al., 2024). For example, one of the classes collaborating with our team has been reading *Summer of the Mariposas* by Guadalupe García McCall (2012), a telling of Homer's *Odyssey* but centering on five Mexican-American sisters who begin a magical journey transporting a corpse they have discovered. Some of the data representations are simple frequency counts of words (see Figure 4.3), but serve as starting points for class and small group discussion about what may or may not be happening in different chapters of the book or what are important themes, symbols, or motifs.

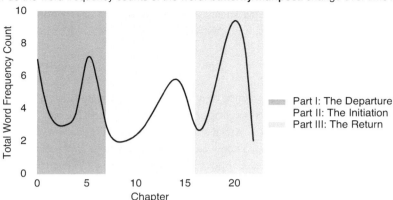

Figure 4.3 A data visualization from the ELAlytics project, showing the appearance of the word butterfly (or mariposas) across different parts of the book, *Summer of the Mariposas*.

Beyond building more comfort with data and showing glimpses of how the humanities can involve data work, *ELAlytics* is also motivated by the idea that a healthy skepticism and multiple approaches to making sense of a situation are useful. Sometimes the data in a visualization provide important new insight. Sometimes it could be misleading. These are importance competences for students to develop when thinking about data, and they appear to be accessible (Coelho et al., 2024). As this is situated in ELA classrooms, this work also centers ELA educator goals such as text comprehension, recognizing authorial craft, and understanding narrative arc structures but develops new pathways where data visualization can be supportive.

Social Studies

Social studies classes have opportunities to use data, although, based on analyses of curriculum (Shreiner, 2020), they are not heavily pursued or supported. In some respects, this is an especially urgent area of need. As Shreiner and Guzdial (2024) have observed:

> While some people need to interpret a scatterplot in *Nature*, most people try to get information relevant to their civic and social lives from infographics in *USA Today* and *The New York Times*. Social studies

teachers are presumably equipped through their training and background knowledge as social studies teachers to teach equity-driven, justice-oriented data literacy that is too often missing from curricula in other subjects.

(pp. 133–134)

In Shreiner and Guzdial's work, they have taken seriously that social studies classrooms and educators are important spaces for data literacy (even noting that this is prominent in social studies education standards—see Shreiner (2020)). Some of the approaches that they have noted include using scaffolded coding support (i.e., support in using JavaScript) to create visualizaitons or free platforms like CODAP for rendering data visualizations without requiring code. They have also engaged in participatory design with social studies teachers to develop an environment called DV4L to facilitate social studies data visualization creation in the context of a driving question and with "slow reveals" of graphical components to both ease and pace reading and interpreting data visualizations in social studies classrooms (Shreiner & Guzdial, 2024).

There are other forms of support available. Data journalism and data infographics (e.g., Polman & Gebre, 2015) in news media are important resources, and examples include "What's going on in this Graph"[1] in the *New York Times*, which has been used by some teachers to look at current events and topics with data. Some supports are available. A number of free resources are available online. For teachers, the Census Bureau provides regular *Statistics in Schools* activities using current data (https://www.census.gov/programs-surveys/sis.html). To give a flavor for this, here is a list of some of the 2024 lessons and activities available for high school (note that there are elementary and middle school lessons too).

- Exploring 19th-century population growth through interactive maps
- Antebellum Economy—understanding employment in 1850
- Trends in Congressional Apportionment
- The Highway System—its development and impact on the United States

Another interesting effort to integrate social studies has explored migration patterns and representation using electronic textiles. In this project, done with middle school students, questions about the reduction of Indigenous people's land over time are posed and then represented with fabric and light representations of Indigenous land over time (Hansen et al., 2024). This endeavor broaches not only interests of data science education in social studies, but maker education and its connections to social studies as well.

Science

Science has strong data connections and is also an intriguing area for data scientific work given the increasing ability to use large amounts of data from sensor networks and multi-lab collaborations (Sagrans et al., 2022). Indeed, sensors in science classrooms such as those made by Vernier or Pasco have compelling research bases for classroom use. This has continued into contemporary versions which integrate with a variety of data analysis applications (Hardy et al., 2020).

Data analysis and interpretation, as well as core statistical ideas used for working with data, are an explicit part of the Next Generation Science Standards. There is still more to explore with how to integrate data science beyond these ideas that have long been part of statistics education. The data cycle (see Chapter 2 and Figure 4.3) aligns well. However, there are few instances of machine learning applications used in K-12 science classrooms, although there is a transformation afoot in the professional sciences due to the increased availability of data and computing power.

Still, simply considering a process orientation of data science, there are some important efforts under way to support such investigative data work including through programs like *Data Nuggets* (Schultheis & Kjelvik, 2015). *Data Nuggets* (datanuggets.org) is a project based out of Michigan State University which connects professional biological science research and data sets to classrooms for use. An example of this includes "Trees and the City" featuring scientist Adrienne Keller from the University of Minnesota. This specific nugget activity involves looking at spatial data of tree cover and examining demographic distributions, including areas that are more densely populated by people of color and analyzing line graphs of tree cover, income, and racial composition of neighborhoods. Students are asked to think through what are the key variables, articulate claims and provide evidence in support of their claims, and articulate future questions to investigate with more data in the future. "Trees and the City" represents one example from a growing repository that includes over 100 marine life, plant ecology, climate change, animal behavior, and pollution data investigations. *Data Nuggets* also provides links to popular tools and free data sets available online for motivated classrooms to use that are not tied to specific lessons.

In younger grades, some activities to pursue data investigations in school that are supportive of science learning goals have also been designed and pursued. Classic among these is work led by Lehrer and Schauble (2002) who pioneered forms of design research that invited elementary students to perform "Data modeling" (Lehrer & Romberg, 1996). Data modeling is an iterative process of posing questions, devising strategies for getting and representing data, posing new questions, and ultimately participating in scientific modeling practices that involves refining understandings and approximations that help explain phenomena in the world. For instance, "fast plants" have been used in several of these studies to ask questions about variation due to measurement and error and think about distributional properties of a data set (Lehrer & Schauble, 2004).

Computer Science

Computer science has a strong affinity for data science, although it is entirely possible to focus on computer science instruction without working with the types of data that are heavily represented in data science. Computer science often involves work with data structures, but specific forms like data frames, tables, and tibbles are more specific to data science work (see Chapter 2). However, there are efforts to embed rich data experiences in high school computer science instruction. One example comes from the *Exploring Computer Science* (ECS) curriculum based out of the University of Oregon (Goode et al., 2012). Their curriculum, used by schools and teachers across the country, includes a number of units that explore topics like human-computer interaction, physical computing, web design, and robotics. One unit of ECS in particular focuses on computing and data analysis and has students work with categorical and continuous variables, Center for Disease Control data, and common data representations like histograms. This curriculum is also amenable for use in Career and Technical Education programs.

Arts

Data visualization has been explored with arts integration. At the University of Pennsylvania, Stornaiuolo (2020) has reported on a study of the artistic work around data done by high school students in a media maker space.

With the school media arts teacher, the students in this East Coast urban high school participated in an extended project of collecting and analyzing personally meaningful data and constructing stories around the data through artistic expression. Their products were then printed onto T-shirts. Some examples of data stories include web traffic to their own personal commercial websites, a personal love of anime, or their feelings about some of their interpersonal relationships over time. The entire experience positioned students as authors and storytellers through collection, interpretation, and visualization of their data.

At New York University and Fordham University, a team has been working with art teachers to create arts-integrated data science experiences where students emphasize ideas such as novel data visualizations using materials such as string and crayons (Matuk et al., 2021), using photographs as sources of data, or creating "data comics" that help students to tell stories about their data (Matuk et al., 2024; Vacca et al., 2022).

Members of that team also developed and are actively exploring intersections between data and dance with a school in the Midwest. Through different choreographies and movements, dancers expressed quantities and stories typically represented in graphs and data visualizations. For example, middle school students choreographed moves to express differences in women's rights around the world through seated and rising body positions or *Minecraft* viewership over time on *Twitch* that incorporated robot-like body movements akin to the characters in the game.

Music is also a popular art of great interest for students, and building on that interest has been an appealing way to connect to interests young people have in popular music. Basu et al. (2020) had designed a game experience for middle school students to explore data science and make decisions in the role of a music producer. The gameplay also supported formative assessment to gauge intuitions and progress regarding data and computing. Astrapoopour Irgens et al. (2023) pursued the topic of music and the music industry in an elementary music classroom, demonstrating how the cultural relevance of popular music could create pathways for young students to engage in data practices.

Health, Physical Education, and Recess

While it had not been the intentional focus, work done by my team with upper elementary and middle grade students using data from what are now broadly called "activity trackers" naturally extended to students' questions about recess and physical education (PE) class. In this work, taking place in the early 2010s, we provided students with various activity tracker wearable devices that could collect data on steps, heart rate, or calories. This led to a number of interesting explorations and opportunities for students to build more knowledge from the playground and play fields at their school, including investigations on the differences in activity levels between playing (American) football and soccer (Lee, Drake, Cain, & Thayne, 2015), four square play behavior (Lee et al., 2021), and their own invented obstacle courses (Lee & Thomas, 2011) during recess or other parts of the school day such as PE class. The ability to work with a device that could ostensibly measure steps led to a number of interesting questions central to data literacy and data science about the nature of measurement, accuracy, and trustworthiness (Lee, Drake, & Williamson, 2015). One especially noteworthy investigation came about when discussing the impact of jump rope on step counts and led students to puzzle through whether jumping would register as a step or not in a step-counting device (Drake et al., 2017).

In recent years, a novel project using a different activity tracker technology in Cyprus, Agesilaou and Kyza (2022) has also focused on students using the technology as a stimulus to motivate thinking about data. They designed classroom instruction for fifth and sixth-grade students that relied on activity tracker technology and questions about physical activity and data along with health and nutrition decisions. A compelling area of inquiry from this Cypriot study was the ways in which it centered a critical reflection on privacy and ethics associated with this technology as it has become increasingly ubiquitous. From this work, they have been developing frameworks for helping students to think about data privacy and ownership that extend beyond data on physical activity (see also Chapter 3 for more discussion of this project).

As will be discussed in Chapter 5, other notable health and physical activity programs that connect to data literacy and data science education appear in non-school settings too.

Educational Technologies

The use of technology has been encouraged in statistics education as it can enable rapid exploration of sampling and ways of manipulating data to see patterns. Technology supports for data science education have been around for decades and have been informed by statistics education research. Early on, specialized applets were created to show frequency plots and distribution graphically and help students move through the four different lenses on data (see Chapter 3).

Dynamic Drag-and-Drop Data Visualization Tools

Another paradigm that emerged involved showing the manipulation of specific data cases that had multiple attributes and simultaneously showing plots and individual data records. Among the earliest was a tool called Tabletop (Hancock et al., 1992) that helped to make groups of individual icons that each represented a record in a larger database. Through various groupings and segmentations, attributes could be organized visually in tables, graphs, or other common plots. This particular software made it possible for a kind of data work that Erickson et al. (2019) call "data moves" easier to perform. To understand data moves, Erickson offers the metaphor of a stack of cards. With data moves, one performs operations on that stack as part of their inquiry process. If we were talking about a 52-card deck of playing cards, there might be moves to filter out all the red cards and then of those, place the face cards in order in alphabetical order. If instead of playing cards we consider each record in a database as constituting and contributing to the values recorded on the card, then there are moves such as filtering (e.g., focus only on data related to cats from an animal shelter database), grouping (split into groups based on coat color), and calculating (compute the average time before adoption in order to see if there is an association between coat color and speed of adoptability).

Extending that model of cards and visualization, tools such as *TinkerPlots* (intended for elementary and middle grade users, see Figure 4.4) (Konold & Miller, 2005) and *Fathom* (intended for high school users) (Finzer et al., 2002) had been developed by education researchers and technologists. These enabled a number of data moves, drag-and-drop controls, and adding annotations and text fields, and performing a variety of calculations through a pre-set menu and buttons and also through a script editor.

92 Advancing Data Science Education in K-12

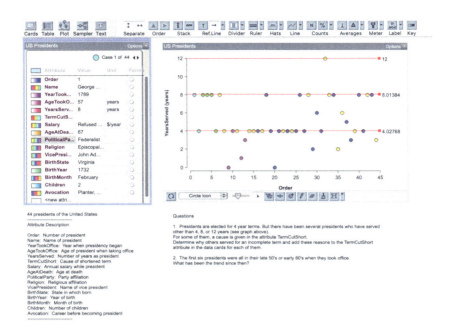

Figure 4.4 TinkerPlots data visualization showing data for the sample data set about US presidents as of 2020.

Figure 4.5 CODAP's interface and data visualization showing the sample data set on roller coasters.

Over the last decade, some of the individuals who were involved in the research and design of tools like this helped to develop a free online system that had similar capabilities called CODAP, shown in Figure 4.5. Given more students using online apps for their work rather than desktop ones, this was a sensible move. CODAP is open source and provides capabilities to connect and store projects in the cloud, and it is actively undergoing research-based enhancements and refinements with ways to organize and represent data and support learning. Some of these enable the creation of data stories that help students to record their investigative process (Wilkerson & Laina, 2018). Others, which had appeared in earlier tools, include generating probability simulations. Some games had also been developed to help students to situate statistical ideas in an activity or task, such as in a game (see Figure 4.6). Commercially, a very similar feature set appears in *TuvaLabs*[2'] online product.

Figure 4.6 One of CODAP's data games in which the player tries to figure out a strategy for beating a character at Roshambo in order to save an innocent dog.

Other Pedagogical Data Analysis Tools

The drag-and-drop manipulation of individual data points (or cases) paradigm is a well-established one but not the only one. For example, a pedagogical tool for data analysis called *DataClassroom*, which has a partnership with the *Data Nuggets* project mentioned above, allows the selection of data sets and interface wizards that guide through a selection of statistical tests and the production of common data visualizations. *DataClassroom* operates in a "freemium" model where some features are available, but additional ones require a license.

Also, it should be no surprise that spreadsheet software, such as *Microsoft Excel* or *Google Sheets*, are perhaps the most widely recognized and heavily used data analysis systems. While there are coding languages (e.g., *R*, *Python*), apps (e.g., *RStudio*, *Tableau*), and notebook environments (e.g., *Jupyter Notebooks*) to support data analysis, spreadsheets are not at any risk of losing pervasiveness or relevance. Given their availability and familiarity, spreadsheet productivity apps are often a starting place and are still capable of doing advanced analyses. One only needs to check message boards for data scientists to see that they are still in regular use, although for maximum flexibility, other tools are preferred. Teachers who wish to work with data in their classrooms will often default to spreadsheets, and it is still the core data tool of many workplaces. Indeed, using more familiar spreadsheet tools in schools might demystify data science and help it move away from an image of being esoteric.

Some bespoke digital data exploration environments have been created. *Databasic.io* is a tool for educators to use that will explore data work. For instance, databasic includes a word frequency analyzer that students can use to compare popular musical artists song lyrics in terms of common words and common bigrams. It can produce quick data plots from an uploaded csv file to help students gain an initial understanding of what might be discoverable in a given file. There is even a tool to show cosine similarity across two text files.

Coding for Data

To facilitate the generation of code, some have been working on a data-focused block-based approach that is popular in a number of youth-facing coding tools. For example, in the *Scratch* coding environment, data has code blocks that were developed and studied by Dasgupta and Hill (2017) so that students could perform queries and produce visualizations of block usage data. Building on the *Snap!* Programming language, *NetsBlox* provides users with blocks and the ability to make remote calls to obtain popular data sets such as most popular news articles in the *New York Times* or movie databases and also analyze those data in CODAP or other tools (Grover et al., 2024). Another interesting block-based data programming environment called *PlayData*, currently built as an extension to *Scratch*, helps students to import data sets and create authentic data visualizations (Fernandez et al., 2023). Increasingly, versions of comparable tools, block-based, visualization-friendly intermediary programming tools that use API (Application Programming Interface) calls (e.g., Walker et al., 2024; Weintrop & Israel-Fishelson, 2024), are appearing and are poised to be a major area for future technology design and improvement.

Teachers Learning to Teach about Data

To bring data science education to K-12 classrooms means that there must also be work done to support teachers in learning how to facilitate or lead data science instruction. However, teaching data science is not a typical part of a teacher preparation program. It is also an area where there has been some literature documenting teacher unease with various data, probability, or statistical ideas as they had not been part of rich instruction on those topics in their own development (Makar & Confrey, 2004; Stohl, 2005). While researchers and designers can put in a great deal of time collaborating with schools to ensure that interesting curricula and tools are developed, they will ultimately need non-researcher, non-developer human support to implement. That means teachers and the ways to help them get comfortable teaching with and about data must be a focus for data science education. Additionally, classroom teachers are a constant source of innovation and creation and will be acting as designers in their own right (Brown & Edelson, 2003), crafting lessons and activities to be most appropriately suited for their respective classrooms. While there is yet to be a data science requirement for teacher education, what are some of the things that are appearing on the horizon for teachers?

Even though there is not a requirement for teacher preparation courses about data science, there has been some experimentation. Drawing from my own experiences, I have designed a pre-service teacher education elective on the teaching of data science that emphasized teaching with and about data across subject areas (Lee, 2024). The design of the course involves having teachers participate in their own quantified self-*Dear Data* (Lupi & Posavec, 2016) experience, examining critical concerns about data, and designing their own lessons for use in their future teaching. Some novel activities have included integrations of digital humanities by looking at quantitative analyses of texts as part of high school English class or looking at climate data in new ways in science class (Figure 4.7).

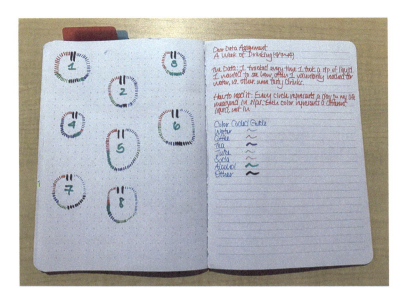

Figure 4.7 A pre-service teacher education student's quantified self-*Dear Data* project. This student tracked all the different sips of beverages she had taken over the course of eight days.

For currently practicing teachers, learning opportunities for teaching data science as professional development can be viewed as too niche for a full school or district commitment, although some pursue professional learning experiences from organizations like *Dataspire* (dataspire.org), which offers data-focused professional development and coaching with an awareness that teachers may lack comfort with these topics. Absent school or district-wide commitments for professional development programs focusing on teaching of data, it becomes incumbent upon motivated teachers to seek other resources on their own. Some teachers are drawn to new K-12 data science curricula that provide their own summer professional development programs for interested teachers (e.g., Gould et al., 2017). Others who are not adopting a specific data science curriculum may pursue online learning experiences, such as MOOCS (Massive Open Online Courses) (Hollebrands & Lee, 2020), or online modules that introduce current pedagogical data analysis tools (such as CODAP), and integrate them into a range of learning management systems (Lee, Hudson, Casey, Mojica, & Harrison, 2021).

Figure 4.8 A data discussion depiction for English Language Arts teachers who are showing frequency word clouds to their students but are not familiar with how to help students to use these and understand them as data. Production support from Elizabeth Finlayson Harris.

Other ways of supporting teachers, especially outside of mathematics, is to focus on professional learning in other subject areas. In the context of high school biology instruction, data and bioinformatics became a topic for high school teachers to explore and further develop their own pedagogical content knowledge related to data (Miller et al., 2021). In work with English Language Arts teachers who are new to teaching about data and using data as a resource for literary education, we have been developing specialized educative curriculum materials to illustrate what teaching with data can look like in a scene-by-scene way (see Figure 4.8).

Accessibility

An area in need of more attention and work for data science education research is for students with learning differences and learning disabilities. There are some new interesting lines of work emerging. For blind and low vision (BLV) learners, different forms of data visualization representations have been developed. Approaches include improvements in tactile graphics such as packages that can help convert common data graphics from *R* into Braille and packages that help with the sonification of data representations (Seo et al., 2024). Another approach is to build custom objects, like an interactive desktop balance board where BLV students can create 3-D representations of data distributions and develop their intuitions about measures of center through manipulation and sound (Fan et al., 2024).

Another approach to be more inclusive of neurodiversity has been to explore movement and balance of the body. Tancredi et al. (2022) have been designing ways to leverage fidgeting and self-regulative movements for K-12 students with learning differences to sit on and adjust a balance board to produce different types of line graphs, coordinating their movements with the graphical representation conventions. More work should be done in the future—especially as data science education seeks to broaden access and participation as well as equip all people to be able to think carefully about data.

Notes

1 https://www.nytimes.com/column/whats-going-on-in-this-graph.
2 https://tuvalabs.com.

References

Agesilaou, A., & Kyza, E. A. (2022). Whose data are they? Elementary school students' conceptualization of data ownership and privacy of personal digital data. *International Journal of Child-Computer Interaction, 33*, 100462. https://doi.org/10.1016/j.ijcci.2022.100462

Arastoopour Irgens, G., Herro, D., Fisher, A., Adisa, I., & Abimbade, O. (2023). Bop or flop?: Integrating music and data science in an elementary classroom. *The Journal of Experimental Education, 92*(2), 262–286. https://doi.org/10.1080/00220973.2023.2201570

Bargagliotti, A., Franklin, C., Arnold, P., Gould, R., Johnson, S., Perez, L., & Spangler, D. (2020). *Pre-K-12 Guidelines for Assessment and Instruction in Statistics Education (GAISE) report II*. Retrieved from https://www.amstat.org/asa/files/pdfs/GAISE/GAISEIIPreK-12_Full.pdf

Basu, S., Disalvo, B., Rutstein, D., Xu, Y., Roschelle, J., & Holbert, N. (2020). *The role of evidence centered design and participatory design in a playful assessment for computational thinking about data.* Paper presented at the Proceedings of the 51st ACM Technical Symposium on Computer Science Education, Portland, OR. https://doi.org/10.1145/3328778.3366881

Boaler, J., Conte, K., Cor, K., Dieckmann, J. A., LaMar, T., Ramirez, J., & Selbach-Allen, M. (in press). Studying the opportunities provided by an applied high school mathematics course: Explorations in data science. *Journal of Statistics and Data Science Education,* 1–20. https://doi.org/10.1080/26939169.2024.2333735

Brown, M., & Edelson, D. (2003). *Teaching as design: Can we better understand the ways in which teachers use materials so we can better design materials to support their change in practice?* Design Brief. Evanston, IL: Northwestern University.

Chao, J., Ellis, R., Jiang, S., Rosé, C., Finzer, W., Tatar, C., ... Wiedemann, K. (2024). Exploring artificial intelligence in English language arts with StoryQ. *Proceedings of the AAAI Conference on Artificial Intelligence, 37*(13), 15999–16003. https://doi.org/10.1609/aaai.v37i13.26899

Coelho, R., Levine, S., Abdi, D., Phalen, L., Harris, L., Demszky, D., & Lee, V. R. (2024). Middle school students engagement with quantitative data representations of fictional texts. In R. Lindgren, T. I. Asino, E. A. Kyza, C. K. Looi, D. T. Keifert, & E. Suárez (Eds.), *Proceedings of the 18th International Conference of the Learning Sciences - ICLS 2024* (pp. 1398–1401). Buffalo, NY: International Society of the Learning Sciences.

Dasgupta, S., & Hill, B. M. (2017). Scratch community blocks: Supporting children as data scientists. In *Proceedings of the 2017 CHI Conference on Human Factors in Computing Systems* (pp. 3620–3631). Denver, CO: ACM.

Drake, J., Cain, R., & Lee, V. R. (2017). From wearing to wondering: Treating wearable activity trackers as tools for inquiry. In I. Levin & D. Tsybulsky (Eds.), *Optimizing STEM education with advanced ICTs and simulations* (pp. 1–29). Hershey, PA: IGI Global.

Erickson, T., Wilkerson, M., Finzer, W., & Reichsman, F. (2019). Data moves. *Technology Innovations in Statistics Education, 12*(1). Retrieved from https://escholarship.org/uc/item/0mg8m7g6

Fan, D., Kim, G. S.-H., Tomassetti, O., Patel, S. N., O'Modhrain, S., Lee, V., & Follmer, S. (2024/under review). *Tangible stats: An embodied and multimodal platform for teaching data and statistics to blind and low vision students.* Paper presented at the CHI 2024, Hawai'i.

Fernandez, C., Lopes, R. D. D., & Blikstein, P. (2023). *Programming representations: Uncovering the process of constructing data visualizations in a block-based programming environment.* Paper presented at the Proceedings of the 2023 Symposium on Learning, Design and Technology, Evanston, IL. https://doi.org/10.1145/3594781.3594783

Finzer, W., Erickson, T., & Binker, J. (2002). *Fathom dynamic statistics software.* Emeryville, CA: Key Curriculum Press.

Gomez, L. M., Fishman, J. B., & Pea, D. R. (1998). The CoVis project: Building a large-scale science education testbed*. *Interactive Learning Environments, 6*(1–2), 59–92. https://doi.org/10.1076/ilee.6.1.59.3608

Goode, J., Chapman, G., & Margolis, J. (2012). Beyond curriculum: The exploring computer science program. *ACM Inroads, 3*(2), 47–53.

Gould, R., Bargagliotti, A., & Johnson, T. (2017). An analysis of secondary teachers' reasoning with participatory sensing data. *Statistics Education Research Journal, 16*(2), 305–334.

Gould, R., Machado, S., Johnson, T. A., & Molynoux, J. (2018). *Introduction to data science v 5.0*. Los Angeles, CA: UCLA Center X.

Grover, S., Jean, D., Broll, B., Cateté, V., Gransbury, I., Ledeczi, A., & Barnes, T. (2024). Design of tools and learning environments for equitable computer science + data science education. In C. Tofel-Grehl & E. Schanzer (Eds.), *Improving equity in data science* (pp. 57–91). New York, NY: Routledge.

Hamilton, M., Clarke-Midura, J., Shumway, J. F., & Lee, V. R. (2020). An emerging Technology report on computational toys in early childhood. *Technology, Knowledge and Learning, 25*(1), 213–224. https://doi.org/10.1007/s10758-019-09423-8

Hancock, C., Kaput, J. J., & Goldsmith, L. T. (1992). Authentic inquiry with data: Critical barriers to classroom implementation. *Educational Psychologist, 27*(3), 337–364.

Hansen, T., Searle, K., Jiang, M., & Barker, M. (2024). Shrinking lands and growing perspectives: Affordances of data science literacy during a culturally responsive maker project. In C. Tofel-Grehl & E. Schanzer (Eds.), *Improving equity in data science* (pp. 37–56). New York, NY: Routledge.

Hardy, L., Dixon, C., & Hsi, S. (2020). From data collectors to data producers: Shifting students' relationship to data. *Journal of the Learning Sciences, 20*(1), 104–126. https://doi.org/10.1080/10508406.2019.1678164

Hollebrands, K. F., & Lee, H. S. (2020). Effective design of massive open online courses for mathematics teachers to support their professional learning. *ZDM, 52*(5), 859–875. https://doi.org/10.1007/s11858-020-01142-0

Horton, N. J., Chao, J., Palmer, P., & Finzer, W. (2023). How learners produce data from text in classifying clickbait. *Teaching Statistics, 45*(S1), S93–S103. https://doi.org/10.1111/test.12339

Jiang, S., Lee, V. R., & Rosenberg, J. M. (2022). Data science education across the disciplines: Underexamined opportunities for K-12 innovation. *British Journal of Educational Technology, 53*(2), 1073–1079. https://doi.org/10.1111/bjet.13258

Konold, C., & Miller, C. (2005). *TinkerPlots. Dynamic data exploration. Statistics software for middle school curricula*. Emeryville, CA: Key Curriculum Press.

Lee, V. R. (2024). Humanistic pre-service data science teacher education across the disciplines. In C. Tofel-Grehl & E. Schanzer (Eds.), *Improving Equity in Data Science: Re-Imagining the Teaching and Learning of Data in K-16 Classrooms* (pp. 112–132). New York: Routledge.

Lee, H. S., Hudson, R., Casey, S., Mojica, G., & Harrison, T. (2021). Online curriculum modules for preparing teachers to teach statistics: Design, implementation, and results. In K. Hollebrands, R. Anderson, & K. Oliver (Eds.), *Online learning in mathematics education* (pp. 65–93). Cham: Springer International Publishing.

Lee, V. R., Abdi, D., Coelho, R., Bywater, C., Levine, S., & Demszky, D. (2024). Identifying pedagogical opportunities for text data visualizations in English language arts through co-design. In R. Lindgren, T. I. Asino, E. A. Kyza, C. K. Looi, D. T. Keifert, & E. Suárez (Eds.), *Proceedings of the 2024 International Conference of the Learning Sciences* (pp. 2201–2022). Buffalo, NY: International Society of the Learning Sciences.

Lee, V. R., Drake, J., Cain, R., & Thayne, J. (2015). Opportunistic uses of the traditional school day through student examination of fitbit activity tracker data. In M. U. Bers & G. Revelle (Eds.), *Proceedings of the 14th International Conference on Interaction Design and Children* (pp. 209–218). Boston, MA: ACM.

Lee, V. R., Drake, J., Cain, R., & Thayne, J. (2021). Remembering what produced the data: Reflective reconstruction in the context of a 'quantified self' elementary data and statistics unit. *Cognition & Instruction, 39*(4), 367–408. https://doi.org/10.1080/07370008.2021.1936529

Lee, V. R., Drake, J., & Williamson, K. (2015). Let's get physical: K-12 Students using wearable devices to obtain and learn about data from physical activities. *TechTrends, 59*(4), 46–53. https://doi.org/10.1007/s11528-015-0870-x

Lee, V. R., & Thomas, J. M. (2011). Integrating physical activity data technologies into elementary school classrooms. *Educational Technology Research and Development, 59*(6), 865–884. https://doi.org/10.1007/s11423-011-9210-9

Lehrer, R., & Romberg, T. A. (1996). Exploring children's data modeling. *Cognition & Instruction, 14*(1), 69–108.

Lehrer, R., & Schauble, L. (2002). *Investigating real data in the classroom: Expanding children's understanding of math and science*. New York, NY: Teachers College Press.

Lehrer, R., & Schauble, L. (2004). Modeling natural variation through distribution. *American Education Research Journal, 41*(3), 635–679.

Lupi, G., & Posavec, S. (2016). *Dear data*. New York, NY: Princeton Architectural Press.

Makar, K., & Confrey, J. (2004). Secondary teachers' statistical reasoning in comparing two groups. In D. Ben-Zvi & J. Garfield (Eds.), *The challenge of developing statistical literacy, reasoning and thinking* (pp. 353–373). Dordrecht, NL: Springer.

Matuk, C., DesPortes, K., Amato, A., Silander, M., Vacca, R., Vasudevan, V., & Woods, P. J. (2021). Challenges and opportunities in teaching and learning data literacy through art. In E. de Vries, Y. Hod, & J. Ahn (Eds.), *15th International Conference of the Learning Sciences (ICLS)* (pp. 681–684). Bochum: ISLS.

Matuk, C., Vacca, R., Amato, A., Silander, M., DesPortes, K., Woods, P. J., & Tes, M. (2024). Promoting students' informal inferential reasoning through arts-integrated data literacy education. *Information and Learning Sciences, 125*(3/4), 163–189. https://doi.org/10.1108/ILS-07-2023-0088

McCall, G. G. (2012). *Summer of the Mariposas*. New York, NY: Lee & Low Books.

Miller, K., Yoon, S., Shim, J., & Cottone, A. (2021). Integrating data literacy into secondary school science: An exploratory study of a pilot professional development. In E. de Vries, Y. Hod, & J. Ahn (Eds.), *Proceedings of the 15th International Conference of the Learning Sciences - ICLS 2021* (pp. 781–784). Bochum: International Society of the Learning Sciences.

Mokros, J., & Russell, S. J. (1995). Children's concepts of average and representativeness. *Journal for Research in Mathematics Education, 26*(1), 20–39.

Papert, S. (1980). *Mindstorms: children, computers, and powerful ideas*. New York, NY: Basic Books.

Podworny, S., Fleischer, Y., Hüsing, S., Biehler, R., Frischemeier, D., Höper, L., & Schulte, C. (2021). *Using data cards for teaching data based decision trees in middle school*. Paper presented at the 21st Koli Calling International Conference on Computing Education Research (Koli Calling '21), Joensuu, Finland.

Polman, J. L., & Gebre, E. H. (2015). Towards critical appraisal of infographics as scientific inscriptions. *Journal of Research in Science Teaching, 52*(6), 868–893. https://doi.org/10.1002/tea.21225

Rubin, A. (2020). Learning to reason with data: How did we get here and what do we know? *Journal of the Learning Sciences, 20*(1), 154–164. https://doi.org/10.1080/10508406.2019.1705665

Rubin, A., & Mokros, J. (1998). *Data: Kids, cats, and ads.* White Plains, NY: Dale Seymour Publications.

Sagrans, J., Mokros, J., Voyer, C., & Harvey, M. (2022). Data science meets science teaching. *The Science Teacher, 89*(3), 64–69.

Schultheis, E. H., & Kjelvik, M. K. (2015). Data nuggets: Bringing real data into the classroom to unearth students' quantitative inquiry skills. *The American Biology Teacher, 77*(1), 19–29. https://doi.org/10.1525/abt.2015.77.1.4

Seo, J., Xia, Y., Lee, B., Mccurry, S., & Yam, Y. J. (2024). MAIDR: Making statistical visualizations accessible with multimodal data representation. In *Proceedings of the chi Conference on Human Factors in Computing Systems*, Honolulu, HI. https://doi.org/10.1145/3613904.3642730

Shreiner, T. L. (2020). Data-literate citizenry: How US state standards address data and data visualizations in social studies. *Information and Learning Sciences, 121*(11/12), 909–931. https://doi.org/10.1108/ILS-03-2020-0054

Shreiner, T. L., & Guzdial, M. (2024). Everyday equitable data literacy is best in Social Studies: STEM can't do what we can do. In C. Tofel-Grehl & E. Schanzer (Eds.), *Improving equity in data science* (pp. 133–150). New York, NY: Routledge.

Son, J. Y., Blake, A. B., Fries, L., & Stigler, J. W. (2021). Modeling first: Applying learning science to the teaching of introductory statistics. *Journal of Statistics and Data Science Education, 29*(1), 4–21. https://doi.org/10.1080/10691898.2020.1844106

Stohl, H. (2005). Probability in teacher education and development. In G. A. Jones (Ed.), *Exploring probability in school: Challenges for teaching and learning* (pp. 345–366). Dordrecht: Springer.

Stornaiuolo, A. (2020). Authoring data stories in a media makerspace: Adolescents developing critical data literacies. *Journal of the learning sciences, 20*(1), 81–103. https://doi.org/10.1080/10508406.2019.1689365

Tancredi, S., Wang, J., Li, H. T., Yao, C. J., Macfarlan, G., & Ryokai, K. (2022). *Balance Board Math: "Being the graph" through the sense of balance for embodied self-regulation and learning.* Paper presented at the Proceedings of the 21st Annual ACM Interaction Design and Children Conference, Braga, Portugal. https://doi.org/10.1145/3501712.3529743

Tatar, C., Jiang, S., Rosé, C. P., & Chao, J. (2024). Exploring teachers' views and confidence in the integration of an artificial intelligence curriculum into their classrooms: A case study of curricular co-design program. *International Journal of Artificial Intelligence in Education.* https://doi.org/10.1007/s40593-024-00404-2

U.S. Department of Education, Institute of Education Sciences, What Works Clearinghouse (2013). *Elementary School Mathematics intervention report: Investigations in Number, Data, and Space®.* Retrieved from https://whatworks.ed.gov

Used numbers (1989). Palo Alto, CA: Dale Seymour Publications.

Vacca, R., DesPortes, K., Tes, M., Silander, M., Matuk, C., Amato, A., & Woods, P. J. (2022). *"I happen to be one of 47.8%": Social-Emotional and Data Reasoning in Middle School Students' Comics about Friendship.* Paper presented at the Proceedings of the 2022 CHI Conference on Human Factors in Computing Systems, New Orleans, LA. https://doi.org/10.1145/3491102.3502086

Walker, J. T., Barany, A., Barrera, A., Johnson, M. A., & Reza, S. M. (2024). Perspectives on research and practice in and around cultural relevance for pre-college data science in computing. In C. Tofel-Grehl & E. Schanzer (Eds.), *Improving equity in data science* (pp. 12–36). New York, NY: Routledge.

Weintrop, D., & Israel-Fishelson, R. (2024). Bringing students' lives into data science classrooms. *Harvard Data Science Review, 6*(3). https://doi.org/10.1162/99608f92.6d2aec03

Wild, C. J., & Pfannkuch, M. (1999). Statistical thinking in empirical enquiry. *International Statistical Review, 67*(3), 223–248. https://doi.org/10.1111/j.1751-5823.1999.tb00442.x

Wilkerson, M. H., & Laina, V. (2018). Middle school students' reasoning about data and context through storytelling with repurposed local data. *ZDM, 50*(7), 1223–1235. https://doi.org/10.1007/s11858-018-0974-9

Yauney, J., Bartholomew, S. R., & Rich, P. (2023). A systematic review of "Hour of Code" research. *Computer Science Education, 33*(4), 512–544.

Learning Data Science Outside of Schools

5

In 2004, the National Science Foundation funded a science of learning center that studied the social foundations of learning in both formal and informal learning environments—called LIFE (Learning in Informal and Formal Environments). A large amount of research was done that spanned neuroscientific work to work on mathematics learning to work on learning with computational tools. One artifact associated with the LIFE Center was a Lifelong and Lifewide Learning Diagram (LIFE Center, 2005) that depicted the number of waking hours spent in both formal and informal learning environments across the lifespan. What many found striking about this diagram was the sheer extent of the diagram that showed that far more of our time both as young people and throughout the lifespan takes place in informal learning environments. During grades 1–12, young people spent an estimated 18.5% of their waking hours in formal learning environments (and therefore 81.5% in informal learning environments). Simply stated, that meant much more time was spent in "not school". Schools are certainly important and worthy of continued research and investment. However, the work from the LIFE Center was one contributor to an increased attention to learning that takes place outside of schools. While this is a book that is oriented toward data science education in K-12 settings, there is still value in understanding what happens outside of schools—especially as these represent alternative models and also assets for the learning that takes place in schools.

Thus, this chapter is about the research on data learning that takes place outside of schools. As schools are structured currently by grade levels that align with specific ages, our conversations about schools stay in roughly a consistent age band. That is not necessarily the case for informal learning environments where the environment and experience is structured differently

DOI: 10.4324/9781003385264-5

and can involve a lot of individual discretion. A museum, for example, contains exhibits where visitors can spend seconds or many minutes. The exhibits may be engaged individually or with a group. The group can have people who are older and younger. They may revisit the exhibit multiple times or just use it once. It can be part of a school field trip, a summer camp, or a family excursion. While not all of these situations obviously bear on how schools do things, there are ways in which we can be attentive to what people know and how people will engage with data in the settings for which school is ostensibly preparing them.

Museums are far from the only type of informal learning environment, although they are notable as educational institutions that are not schools. While others will be discussed below, I will go ahead and comment quickly on work in museums. Other sections will include libraries, hobby activities including athletics and gaming, community programs, and online with digital media.

Museums

One example of a museum experience that encouraged visitors to think about data is do\cumented in a study by Roberts and Lyons (2020). In their work, they had designed an interactive exhibit called *CoCensus* that encouraged visitors to explore demographic information in census data and visualizations. For example, a geographic map on display can be manipulated by visitors to show information about population density, occupation, residence, heritage, or other information that had been systematically collected over the decades. This type of spatial data analysis is a form of data science work that is being done professionally, often with the aid of geographic information systems.

In the Roberts & Lyon study, they were especially interested in ways that visitors connected themselves and their experiences to the data through the way they talked about the information in the exhibit. This type of talk is one that has been observed among professional scientists (Ochs et al., 1996) and has been a compelling type of conversational exchange for new knowledge development and problem solving (Fauconnier & Turner, 2002). Through a systematic analysis of dozens of visitor conversations with the data, Roberts and Lyons saw there were indeed numerous instances of this way of talking about and understanding the data and that under specific circumstances, they seemed to invite more collaborative learning opportunities.

Another project, also involving Lyons (2015), involved students playing with climate change data by way of physically simulating a polar bear who had to swim from one glacier to another in different decades that had different conditions due to global warming. In this exhibit, visitors even donned bear gloves equipped with accelerometers so that they could feel just how much more work it was (and thus a greater energy demand on the polar bears who would need more food for survival).

At the time of this writing, more current efforts are under way to design museum experiences specifically to help visitors explore ideas related to data and data science that are in development. For example, Andee Rubin of TERC is leading a project to help museum exhibit designers to prototype new data science exhibits to add to their spaces.

Figure 5.1 A Galton board, similar to the large ones that are installed in museums for visitors to interact with and observe.

Given that there are over 35,000 museums in the United States according to the Institute of Museum and Library Services, it is likely some have created experiences for exploring data beyond what I have seen or can report here. For instance, some museums have giant Galton boards (see Figure 5.1 for a small one) that produce an approximation of the normal distribution through random processes—an important topic in probability and statistics, and thus pertinent to data science. As data science education becomes a greater national concern, we should expect that museums will also contribute to the educational experience through creation of exhibits as well as new experiences for visitors and for other educators who go to museums for further professional training (e.g., teachers who participate in professional development programs housed at museums).

Libraries

Libraries have been a topic of special interest for me professionally (Lee & Phillips, 2018), in large part out of appreciation for the welcoming space they provide to any visitor regardless of circumstance. Jennifer Kahn (2020) had done work with an urban library to provide a free program for teens and families to use tools like *Social Explorer* and *GapMinder* and build their "geobiographies" using the data visualizations those tools could produce. Also using census and demographic data from various periods, the teens researched their families' migration history in and throughout the United States and the drivers of relocation. They also added to the library collection by producing recordings of their projects. This approach was another successful one at making data more personally relevant and connecting young people to both family and national history.

In an effort to expand one area of focus for libraries, information literacy, to include data literacy as well, Michigan library and information science experts embarked on a multifaceted project to enhance high school librarians' abilities to teach about data that culminated in the free online book *Data Literacy in the Real World: Conversations and Case Studies*[1] (Fontichiaro et al., 2017). Specific strategies for school librarians are included in another book from that team, *Creating Data Literate Students* (Fontichiaro, Oehrli, & Lennex, 2017). That book includes direct accounts from school librarians and how to work with visualizations with students or even prepare data in spreadsheets for use in library instruction.

The American Library Association, in addition to supporting important work related to reading and literacy (as traditionally conceived in books and periodicals), has prepared resources[2] as well relevant to increasing data literacy (the foundation kind, see Chapter 2), both for librarians themselves who may not feel comfortable with data topics and to help them to promote data literacy as part of their educational offerings in their respective library spaces. In the 2010s, with funding support from Google, they launched the *Libraries Ready to Code* initiative that encouraged a number of libraries to bring computer science and computational thinking topics into their educational offerings through library-based programs. While those did not specifically focus on data science, they were laying some foundations for the computational proficiencies associated with data science.

Hobbies and Interest-Driven Activities

Hobbies are an especially important area to consider for informal learning experiences as they tend to be driven strongly by personal interests. However, the nature of participation in hobbies can be quite complicated and varied given differences across people but also differences in how interactions for the hobby are organized and other contextual circumstances. For example, people can be interested in amateur astronomy but could differ in how they participate based on whether they have the financial means to purchase their own telescope, whether they go to star parties, whether they tend to mentoring and teaching or other activities (Azévedo, 2011, 2013).

Organized Data Science Competitions

There are some contexts in which data are part of the hobby because playing with data is what the enthusiasts like to do. For instance, Kaggle regularly hosts data sets and competitions for data scientists (some with cash prizes that are tens of thousands of dollars, although several explicitly state "knowledge" is the prize—a sufficient motivator for some). Online discussion boards provide resources for data science enthusiasts to engage asynchronously with one another. The American Statistical Association sponsors *DataFest*, which is a 48-hour intensive event for undergraduate students from 40 colleges and universities to analyze data; prizes are awarded for best visualization, insight, or use of external data. A study of group work at DataFest suggests it is indeed a space for collaborative problem solving around open-ended challenges (Noll & Tackett, 2023).

At my own institution, Stanford University, there is a multi-organization initiative known as Women in Data Science (WiDS).[3] Among other activities—like mentorship programs and online trainings—to promote more women participating in data science, WiDS hosts an annual datathon where groups of women working in or interested in the field form teams to use data science in order to make some headway on a major social challenge for which real data exist. The 2024 WiDS datathon, for example, was sponsored by Gilead Sciences and provided large data sets on metastatic breast cancer, treatment duration, and time to adoption in treatment to see where there were inequities in health care. Other datathon topics from WiDS from previous years looked at predictive model building for deforestation, effects of climate change, patient survival prediction in intensive care units, and financial services for the poor. These WiDS datathons last about six weeks, and, as of 2024, have had over 5,000 competitors.

To draw from the conclusions in Noll and Tackett's (2023) study of *DataFest* participation, these are exciting spaces for hobbyists to engage with data science, although they can be ambitious entry points for novices. While some highly motivated individuals could make headway through these, there is still a place for introductory courses and experiences. However, the type of real data work that takes place and the compelling and complex problems that are tackled could be a good model for some of the activities for introductory courses, as this is how data will actually look in science, industry, and other areas of data work.

Quantified Self Community

In 2007, *Wired* editors Gary Wolf and Kevin Kelly coined the phrase "Quantified Self" to refer to the new opportunities brought about by new sensor tools being made widely available to consumers that would enable new examinations of everyday life and experience, importing some of the growing enthusiasm around data and analytics in technology to a broad suite of individual and routine experiences (Wolf, 2010). Wearable technologies such as smart watches and Internet of Things (IoT) devices were growing in visibility. Through platforms like *MeetUp*, interest in the potential to analyze and gain personal insight and share grew such that major cities around the world began forming groups that would give presentations and tips to one another on their own "Quantified Self" projects. A centralized web community was established (quantifiedself.com), and an international conference for both hobbyists and toolmakers was organized for multiple years.

A presentation for a Quantified Self event typically has three questions for presenters to answer:

- What did you do?
- How did you do it?
- What did you learn?

Several videos of quantified self projects were gathered and remain available online. For instance, some projects looked at cholesterol levels while nursing, professional productivity, frequented locations, modes of transportation, blood sugar levels, and what books were read over the course of a year. Academic research developed around and within this community including in the areas of personal precision medicine (Smarr, 2012) and information studies (Choe et al., 2014; Li et al., 2010). Some explorations of the Quantified Self approach, especially with wearable technology, had also been undertaken in K-12 education (Ching & Hagood, 2019; Lee et al., 2016) (disclosure: this had been a core area of research of mine for many years).

There are legitimate critiques of Quantified Self participation, including relatively homogenous demographic participation (predominantly male, white, young to middle-aged, and in urban areas) (Lee, 2014). It can be an expensive hobby to explore. Also, as more commercial technologies appeared, privacy questions grew (Agesilaou & Kyza, 2022). However, in the rapid growth of consumer wearable technologies, the Quantified Self hobby community and convenings were important spaces for tool developers and participants. Arguably, many of the practices of this community have gone mainstream with activity trackers, glucose monitors, and mobile device usage reports on our phones.

Dear Data

Relatedly, a project that had gained popularity commercially and was consolidated in multiple books was *Dear Data* (Lupi & Posavec, 2016, 2018). I tend to view it as a version of Quantified Self activity because it is the individual doing the investigation who is also the subject of the research, although it does not self identify with the quantified self movement. The basic story behind *Dear Data* was a year-long project between two information designers who lived an ocean apart from one another. They took it upon themselves to select a topic for each week from their everyday lives, collect data, and then hand draw a visualization of those data on a postcard that they mailed to each other. Among the topics that were recorded include how many (and what types of) doors they passed through, how and to whom they said goodbye, use of public transportation, time looking at one's self in the mirror, and purchases made. Key to this is the analog representation of data. One value that they emphasized was that these were data investigations that were for the purposes of personal understanding and connection, rather than in search of solutions or efficiencies (perhaps why they never opted to identify with Quantified Self, which does have an optimization disposition as part of it).

The books by Lupi and Posavec (2016, 2018) provide compelling illustrations from their exchanged postcards as well as guidance on how to pursue a similar project from problem selection to data collection to visualization. In Chapter 4, an example of an actual project in this vein appears in Figure 4.7.

Athletics

Athletes, whether recreational, student, or professional, are often working with data in various forms. For one, performance and decisions about placement or winning in competitions rely on some measurement and scoring system. This makes novel statistics such as batting average in baseball or softball valuable to help understand overall hitting capability in those sports. Also, it is difficult to watch a professional sports event on television without a sports commentator trotting out some statistics for specific players, such as third down conversions in rainy weather for a specific quarterback, field goal percentage on home games for basketball, or overall performance in competitions while training with a certain coach. This has become a part of the ways in which sports are understood for consumption purposes. Indeed, the film *Moneyball* based on the book (2004) of the same name by Michael Lewis speaks to the importance of data and analytics to professional sports, especially in the case of an impressive turnaround for the Oakland A's professional baseball team, which lacked high-profile players but did have high-powered statistical analysts. The embrace of data in sports has grown to the level that there is an annual sports analytics conference hosted by the MIT Sloan School of Business that applies data science to athletic and business questions. In addition, there are indications of more casual uses, such as teen basketball players estimating their own shooting percentages (Nasir, 2000).

In one study completed with Joel Drake (Lee & Drake, 2013), we examined how data were collected and used among runners and cyclists for their respective sports. These were some avid adopters of wearable technologies such as heart rate monitors or bicycle computers. While the devices used could be cutting edge, there was a range of data storage systems that included custom software and sometimes just custom notebooks or calendars (see Figure 5.2). Data were gathered to self-monitor progress, calibrate realistic goals, and benchmark major milestones. There were also ways in which data could feel limiting or cumbersome, and thus be excluded from some activities so as to ensure enjoyment of the sport without constant quantification.

For Division I collegiate sports, Tamara Clegg and colleagues at the University of Maryland (Clegg et al., 2023) have studied data use for and among student athletes. Examples of athletic data use in Clegg et al.'s study included examples of athletes and trainers using data for tracking nutrition, analyzing body composition, calculating speeds and heart rates, and using specialty sensors in their uniforms and equipment. This is in addition to film as a specialized form of data that is regularly used to review performance and prepare for competitions. While there are many forms of use, and athletes develop sophisticated understandings of how to interpret and use the data, Clegg et al. similarly found there are important ways in which athletes wish to disconnect from data and exercise some resistance from the larger systems in which the data are used.

Athletics may be a compelling hook for some students interested in data science, but it also shows a very human side of how data are made meaningful and are part of larger communities. Important observations to take from athletics include the situated and contextualized meanings that data take on within complex practices, the valuable embodied insight that athletes have that give them depth of perspective around data, and that there are known ways in which data use needs to be moderated so as to not detract from aspects of the activity that are meaningful or consequential to them.

Learning Data Science Outside of Schools   113

2008 Workouts

Week	Monday	Tuesday	Wednesday	Thursday	Friday	Saturday	Sunday	Week Hours	Total Hours	Goal Hours	Week Miles	Total Miles	Goal Miles
Dec 31	Snow Shoe 105 (2.25)	Running 120 (10.25) Elliptical 30 (1.75) Weights 30 Elliptical 30 (1)				Running 60 (5.25) Shvl Snow 75	Shvl Snow 90	9	9	7	20.5	20.5	20
Jan 7	Running 60 (5)	Shvl Snow 30	Shvl Snow 60	Running 60 (5.5)	Shvl Snow 45	Running 90 (8.5) Weights 45 2"	Shvl Snow 30 Walking 30 (1.5)	7.5	16.5	14	20.5	41	40
Jan 14		Walking 105 (5.75)	Elliptical 30 (1.75) Weights 30	Running 60 (5) Weights 45 2" Shvl Snow 15	Shvl Snow 30	Running 90 (8) Elliptical 30 (1.75)		7.25	23.75	21	22.25	63.25	60
Jan 21	Shvl Snow 75 Running 105 (8.75)			Running 90 (8) Weights 60 2"	Shvl Snow 15	Running 60 (5.5) Elliptical 30 (1.75) Snow Shoe 120 (3)		9.25	33	28	27	90.25	80
Jan 28	Shvl Snow 15			Elliptical 60 (2) Weights 45 2" Shvl Snow 60		Running 90 (8) Snow Shoe 120 (3.5) Deer Fence	Shvl Snow 30 Shvl Snow 15	7.25	40.25	35	13.5	103.75	100
Feb 4	Shvl Snow 15		Shvl Snow 30	Running 60 (5) Snow Shoe 60 (1.75) Country Club Shvl Snow 30		Freeze Your Buns Run 29.12 (3.1) Weights 45 2" Elliptical 30 (1.75)	Walking 45 (2.75) Run/Walk 90 (7)	7.25	47.5	42	21.25	125	120
Feb 11			Shvl Snow 75	Shvl Snow 30 Running 45 (3)		Run/Walk 90 (7) Run/Walk 60 (4) Weights 60 2" Elliptical 30 (1.5)		6.5	54	49	15.5	140.5	140
Feb 18	Running 75 (7.25)			Running 60 (5.25) Elliptical 30 (1.75)		Running 60 (5.25) Elliptical 30 (1.75) Elliptical 30 (1) Weights 45 2"		5.5	59.5	56	22.25	162.75	160
Feb 25				Running 90 (8) Elliptical 75 (4.25)				2.75	62.25	63	12.25	175	180
Mar 3		Walking 75 (4.25)			Run/Walk 75 (6) Walk 45 (2.25)	Running 75 (6.5) Boot Camp 45 Weights 45 2"		6	68.25	70	19	194	200
Mar 10		Elliptical 60 (1.75) Elliptical 60 (3)		Boot Camp 45 Weights 45 2"		Running 75 (6.25) Hill Reps 15 (1.5) Weights 30 Elliptical 30 (1.5)		6	74.25	77	14	208	220
Mar 17	Run/Walk 60	Weights 30	Yard Work 30	Running 60 (5.5)	Running 105 (8.25)	Walk 15 (.5)		8.75	83	84	26.75	234.75	240

Figure 5.2 One runner's self-made and self-maintained workout tables with information he decided to track.

Fantasy Sports and Esports

Related to athletics and data are other digitally mediated sporting and gaming experiences. Fantasy sports is a robust industry where a form of "competitive fandom" (Halverson & Halverson, 2008) can be realized. Enthusiasts can leverage their knowledge of the sport or game and harness domain expertise in ways that allow them to create composite teams that are evaluated based on actual professional athletes' performance. Interestingly, while there are many measures and statistics involved, research on the reasoning processes of fantasy sports participants suggests that there is not a formal use of mathematical techniques—rather, there are informal heuristics that can serve as a strong foundation for future mathematical knowledge development (Smith et al., 2006).

With Fred Poole, now at Michigan State University, I conducted a small study on Esports athletes' use of data (Poole & Lee, 2022). Esports, understood also as competitive videogaming, can be a complex social activity in which a great deal of strategy and team coordination is involved. In observations and interviews with college student Esports athletes, we observed that data retention was not an embedded practice—however, when given the support to retain data and review decision trees developed from their practices and competitions, they would critically reappraise player decisions and strategies. For many gamers, seeing some brief descriptive statistics of performance—such as number of kills, rescues, tokens, and game duration—is common. However, cumulative data are harder to come by. Much of the focus on digitally mediated sports and game experiences suggests that the potential to build on data from those activities is there, although the limited data capture and instructional support for how to work with those data would need to be addressed in order to further enrich these activities as data science learning opportunities.

Data in the Home

Arguably, the home would be another potential venue for informal learning about data, although it has not been studied to the same extent in the academic literature. There are consistently moments that appear in the home where data are mentioned in some way, although it can be part of a commentary about recent things seen in the media (e.g., what temperature records have been broken or what new scientific research finding has come out and been hyped in the news). There are ways in which data are discussed in the context of other activities such as grade point averages and finances. With the increased push toward "smart homes" for those who can afford such technologies, there are some ways in which the regular use of those technologies calibrates specific expectations about data. For instance, despite knowing there are security and privacy risks associated with smart home technologies and associated data, users appeared to be largely unconcerned and very trusting of how data are being handled with commercial IoT (Tabassum et al., 2019).

One study I had done with Ilana Dubovi, now at Tel Aviv University, involved examining how families navigated data in a special case: monitoring and providing care for a child who had type 1 diabetes (T1D) (Lee & Dubovi, 2020). T1D is a lifelong ailment where the body produces little to no insulin, which is an essential hormone required to manage blood sugar levels. Untreated, T1D can lead to serious problems for many organs in the body and can lead to death. To manage T1D, patients need to monitor their blood sugar levels, their diet, their physical activity levels, and their self-administered insulin dosing. For children, this requires a number of calculations and numerical practices that they have not yet mastered, thus making this a more complex caregiving affair.

Through observations and interviews with families, we saw a range of ways in which the datafication of daily life at home was monitored and managed, from continuous estimates of foods to keeping detailed logs to using continuous glucose monitoring technology. Because young children were involved, parents and children found themselves continuously educating others about the disease and the considerations that were necessary for its management. Parents would also deploy novel strategies to help their children learn about the quantities and recognize subjective feelings associated with low or high blood sugar levels and the numerical values that were coming from a blood glucose test so they could have multiple ways of appraising their status. While unusual, we even saw a case where a PhD-trained parent used advanced data science techniques to analyze log data that the family had collected for their son to evaluate the impacts of certain foods, such as pizza, on their child's blood sugar levels.

One observation of note from this work in the home is that deliberate reflection of aggregated data was rare. It is valuable to see there are many ways in which data and conversations appear in the home that can be relevant to build upon in the classroom, but home data conversations are not typically ones where systematic reflections across large sets of data are being done. This seems to be an area where schools can help young people—to navigate the local and global readings of data (Ben-Zvi & Arcavi, 2001).

Participatory Community Data Work

Community engagement with data and data science is one that a number of researchers have also noted with interest. One form is through what has in the past been called "citizen science" where non-scientist members of a community or throughout a large geographical area help collect data from their locales for a larger science endeavor. For example, the Cornell Lab of Ornithology hosts bird monitoring citizen science programs (https://www.birds.cornell.edu/citizenscience) where bird sightings and nesting can be recorded to help monitor migration and prevalence. NASA also hosts citizen science projects for interested individuals, such as one to gather and contribute exoplanet data from personal telescopes or use cell phones to report rain or snow conditions at nearby mountains. By connecting to online resources and helping prepare data, the public has an opportunity to learn more about how data are used in scientific research.

Other forms of community engagement with data can look like advocacy work. For example, Katie Headrick Taylor at the University of Washington had led a project where youth collected GPS data and examined transportation options in their city, finding that it lacked safe biking areas and ultimately taking their findings and data to city leaders to revise development plans (Taylor et al., 2013). In the Boston area, Rahul and Emily Bhargava partnered with a community organization to produce data murals—large painted displays in public spaces that include statistics and infographics about the community members and their concerns (Bhargava et al., 2016). Community data gathering efforts such as a ground-based gathering of information about vacant and abandoned lots have also been another form of community data gathering and advocacy (Meng & DiSalvo, 2018). DiSalvo's lab has other related projects of community data gathering, such as documenting the presence of rats, to support advocacy work to improve the residential conditions of neighborhoods that have been historically overlooked or underserved.

These examples are inspiring with respect to mobilizing communities and helping them to voice their concerns and needs to inspire new city policies. Similar endeavors in classrooms that have comparable models—working with local spatial data and completing field work to enrich data with resident perspectives and concerns—have been pursued (Rubel et al., 2016). It is worth observing that while this is laudable, the ultimate changes at the policy level can be difficult to complete at the time scales of these projects (van Wart et al., 2020). However, these endeavors provide rich local learning opportunities and provide learners with visions of new forms of civic participation that involve data.

Digital Media

Digital media—inclusive of social media and other online information platforms—are an important part of the out-of-school learning ecosystem as people of all ages spend a great deal of time in these spaces to learn and share with one another. Data journalism has grown with interactives in mainstream news sites such as the *New York Times*, but also in data-centric sites such as *The Pudding* (pudding.cool is the web address), which provides novel data visualizations and interactive digital media stories that prominently feature interactive data components. Organizations such as *YR Media* (yrmedia.org) in Oakland have been active in providing young people with support, models, and pathways for media authorship and creation by helping young people to produce podcasts and news articles that get distributed by mainstream media. Included in their work had been a specific focus on helping young people tell data stories and providing online resources and examples such as critical examinations of proctoring software or tools to help people see how powerful and alarming some facial recognition technologies that have been trained on image data have become (see *Erase Your Face* on yrmedia.org).

Social media has been and continues to be where data conversations take place, although these may be very short engagements. During the COVID-19 pandemic, young people were actively using social media to get, share, challenge, and expand on data about how the pandemic and associated restrictions were affecting them and their communities, especially given disparate effects on historically marginalized groups (Calabrese Barton et al., 2021). The pandemic was also an intensive time for data investigation and sense-making by adults (Radinsky & Tabak, 2022) who were continuously scanning and puzzling through new findings and considering carefully their applicability to personal safety decisions. These COVID-19 era examples, aside from showing the breadth of data engagement in the time of a global public health crisis, also illustrated how complex emotions and social relationships mattered in data work.

TikTok is a space for data engagement with some short form videos involving stylized speakers making argumentative points about data. For example, in videos about climate change, creators would often respond to data in the news, talk about changes in weather patterns, and then situate the topic in specific reactions or actions (such as hacks to reduce waste or energy usage) (Nguyen & Parameswaran, 2023). Youth intuitions about algorithms and recommendations from *YouTube* were explored in Delaney et al. (2023). However, while alarm has been expressed about how much youth are using and being affected by social media, youth responses seem to still emphasize enjoyment, reliance, and lack of concern about data privacy. This may be an area for future innovation in K-12 education, both as examples for classes to think through (e.g., how do recommendations work?) and also for preferable and healthy uses of these platforms that are generating huge amounts of data.

Connecting across Settings

The purpose in examining data science education experiences outside of school settings in a book focused on K-12 data science education research was in part to provide inspiration for new things to do in the classroom (Lee, 2015) and also to gain an appreciation for the breadth of data activity and learning opportunities that exist across settings. In recent decades, greater appreciation for how learning takes place across settings, even though we designate schools as an especially important one that exists in a specific place for specific age groups, has grown. This is evidenced in conceptualizations of connected learning, which greatly amplified how young people move across non-school settings to learn different things at different times (Ito et al., 2013). Also relevant is the proposal to examine not just single learning environments, like a classroom, but rather entire learning ecologies to see how different experiences, mentors, and conditions carry across formal, informal, online, and other spaces for learning (Barron, 2006).

It is hard to imagine that schools will cease to exist, but with greater mobility and increased digital connectivity, we can more fully appreciate how the experiences of young people outside of the classroom walls matter. They provide the background knowledge and ways of thinking about the world that form the basis for future understanding. There are other ways to think about the learning that takes place outside of the classroom that is important for those interested in K-12 education. Teachers participate in summer professional development and informal conversations with colleagues and look to social media and online resources to grow in their practice. Many other adults who have finished their formal schooling look to new online experiences professionally, like boot camps and online courses, to learn more about data science. At the same time, some experiences for youth in informal learning environments can bear strong resemblance to or be considered a continuation of a formal learning experience. For example, school field trips and camps can be quite school-like even if they are off school grounds. The boundaries can quickly blur. Thus, it seems worthwhile for anyone interested in data science education—whether it is for the purposes of K-12 classrooms or for settings outside of schools—to be keeping an eye out for what is happening on the other side.

Notes

1 https://quod.lib.umich.edu/m/maize/mpub9970368/1:1/--data-literacy-in-the-real-world-conversations-case-studies?rgn=div1;view=fulltext.
2 https://literacy.ala.org/data-literacy/.
3 https://www.widsworldwide.org.

References

Agesilaou, A., & Kyza, E. A. (2022). Whose data are they? Elementary school students' conceptualization of data ownership and privacy of personal digital data. *International Journal of Child-Computer Interaction, 33*, 100462. https://doi.org/10.1016/j.ijcci.2022.100462

Azévedo, F. (2011). Lines of practice: A practice-centered theory of interest relationships. *Cognition & Instruction, 29*(2), 147–184.

Azévedo, F. S. (2013). The tailored practice of hobbies and its implication for the design of interest-driven learning environments. *Journal of the Learning Sciences*. https://doi.org/10.1080/10508406.2012.730082

Barron, B. (2006). Interest and self-sustained learning as catalysts of development: A learning ecology perspective. *Human Development, 49*(4), 193–224. Retrieved from https://www.karger.com/DOI/10.1159/000094368

Ben-Zvi, D., & Arcavi, A. (2001). Junior high school students' construction of global views of data and data representations. *Educational Studies in Mathematics, 45*(1), 35–65. doi:10.1023/A:1013809201228

Bhargava, R., Kadouaki, R., Bhargava, E., Castro, G., & D'Ignazio, C. (2016). Data murals: Using the arts to build data literacy. *The Journal of Community Informatics, 12*(3).

Calabrese Barton, A., Greenberg, D., Turner, C., Riter, D., Perez, M., Tasker, T., ... Davis, E. A. (2021). Youth critical data practices in the COVID-19 multipandemic. *AERA Open, 7*, 23328584211041631. https://doi.org/10.1177/23328584211041631

Ching, C. C., & Hagood, D. (2019). Activity monitor gaming and the next generation science standards: Students engaging with data, measurement limitations, and personal relevance. *Journal of Science Education and Technology, 28*(6), 589–601. https://doi.org/10.1007/s10956-019-09789-5

Choe, E. K., Lee, N. B., Lee, B., Pratt, W., & Kientz, J. A. (2014). *Understanding quantified-selfers' practices in collecting and exploring personal data.* Paper presented at the Proceedings of the SIGCHI Conference on Human Factors in Computing Systems, Toronto, Ontario, Canada.

Clegg, T. L., Cleveland, K., Weight, E., Greene, D., & Elmqvist, N. (2023). Data everyday as community-driven science: Athletes' critical data literacy practices in collegiate sports contexts. *Journal of Research in Science Teaching, 60*(8), 1786–1816. https://doi.org/10.1002/tea.21842

Delaney, V., Sarin, P., & Lee, V. R. (2023). Students' constructed explanations for how artificial intelligence generates recommendations in YouTube. In *Proceedings of the 17th International Conference of the Learning Sciences - ICLS 2023*. Montreal: ISLS.

Fauconnier, G., & Turner, M. (2002). *The way we think: Conceptual blending and the mind's hidden complexities.* New York, NY: Basic Books.

Fontichiaro, K., Lennex, A., Hoff, T., Hovinga, K., & Oehrli, J. A. (Eds.). (2017). *Data literacy in the real world: Conversations & case studies*. Ann Arbor: Michigan Publishing.

Fontichiaro, K., Oehrli, J. A., & Lennex, A. (Eds.). (2017). *Creating data literate students*. Ann Arbor, MI: Maize Books.

Halverson, E. R., & Halverson, R. (2008). Fantasy baseball: The case for competitive fandom. *Games and Culture, 3*(3–4), 286–308. https://doi.org/10.1177/1555412008317310

Ito, M., Gutierrez, K., Livingstone, S., Penuel, B., Rhodes, J., Salen, K., ... Watkins, S. C. (2013). *Connected learning: An agenda for research and design*. Irvine, CA: Digital Media and Learning Research Hub.

Kahn, J. (2020). Learning at the intersection of self and society: The family geobiography as a context for data science education. *Journal of the Learning Sciences, 20*(1), 57–80. https://doi.org/10.1080/10508406.2019.1693377

Lee, V. R. (2014). What's happening in the quantified self movement? In J. L. Polman, E. A. Kyza, D. K. O'Neill, I. Tabak, W. R. Penuel, A. S. Jurow, K. O'Connor, T. Lee, & L. D'Amico (Ed.), *Learning and becoming in practice: The International Conference of the Learning Sciences (ICLS) 2014* (Vol. 2, pp. 1032–1036). Boulder, CO: ISLS.

Lee, V. R. (2015). Looking at how technology is used with the bodies over there to figure out what could be done with the technology and bodies right here. In V. R. Lee (Ed.), *Learning technologies and the body: Integration and implementation in formal and informal learning environments* (pp. 167–184). New York, NY: Routledge.

Lee, V. R., & Drake, J. (2013). Digital physical activity data collection and use by endurance runners and distance cyclists. *Technology, Knowledge and Learning, 18*(1–2), 39–63. https://doi.org/10.1007/s10758-013-9203-3

Lee, V. R., Drake, J. R., & Thayne, J. L. (2016). Appropriating quantified self technologies to improve elementary statistical teaching and learning. *IEEE Transactions on Learning Technologies, 9*(4), 354–365. https://doi.org/10.1109/TLT.2016.2597142

Lee, V. R., & Dubovi, I. (2020). At home with data: Family engagements with data involved in Type 1 diabetes management. *Journal of the Learning Sciences, 20*(1), 11–31. https://doi.org/10.1080/10508406.2019.1666011

Lee, V. R., & Phillips, A. L. (Eds.). (2018). *Reconceptualizing libraries: Perspectives from the information and learning sciences*. New York, NY: Routledge.

Lewis, M. (2004). *Moneyball: The art of winning an unfair game*. New York, NY: W. W. Norton & Company.

Li, I., Dey, A., & Forlizzi, J. (2010). A stage-based model of personal informatics systems. In *Proceedings of the SIGCHI Conference on Human Factors in Computing Systems* (pp. 557–566). Atlanta, GA: ACM.

LIFE Center (2005). *The LIFE center's lifelong and lifewide diagram*. Retrieved from http://life-slc.org/about/about.html

Lupi, G., & Posavec, S. (2016). *Dear data*. New York, NY: Princeton Architectural Press.

Lupi, G., & Posavec, S. (2018). *Observe, collect, draw!: A visual journal: Discover the patterns in your everyday life*. New York: Princeton Architectural Press.

Lyons, L. (2015). Exhibiting data: Using body-as-interface designs to engage visitors with data visualizations In V. R. Lee (Ed.), *Learning technologies and the body: Integration and implementation in formal and informal learning environments* (pp. 185–200). New York, NY: Routledge.

Meng, A., & DiSalvo, C. (2018). Grassroots resource mobilization through counter-data action. *Big Data & Society, 5*(2), 2053951718796862. https://doi.org/10.1177/2053951718796862

Nasir, N. S. (2000). "Points ain't everything": Emergent goals and average and percent understandings in the play of basketball among African American students. *Anthropology & Education Quarterly, 31*(3), 283–305.

Nguyen, H., & Parameswaran, P. (2023). Meaning making and relatedness: Exploring critical data literacies on social media. *Information and Learning Sciences, 124*(5/6), 149–167. https://doi.org/10.1108/ILS-02-2023-0016

Noll, J., & Tackett, M. (2023). Insights from DataFest point to new opportunities for undergraduate statistics courses: Team collaborations, designing research questions, and data ethics. *Teaching Statistics, 45*(S1), S5–S21. https://doi.org/10.1111/test.12345

Ochs, E., Gonzales, P., & Jacoby, S. (1996). "When I come down I'm in the domain state": Grammar and graphic representation in the interpretive activity of physicists. In E. Ochs, E. Schegloff, & S. Thompson (Eds.), *Interaction and grammar* (pp. 328–369). New York, NY: Cambridge University Press.

Poole, F., & Lee, V. R. (2022). *Esports athletes' sense-making from quantified-self play data.* Paper presented at the Games + Learning + Society, Irvine, CA.

Radinsky, J., & Tabak, I. (2022). Data practices during COVID: Everyday sensemaking in a high-stakes information ecology. *British Journal of Educational Technology, 53*(5), 1221–1243. https://doi.org/10.1111/bjet.13252

Roberts, J., & Lyons, L. (2020). Examining spontaneous perspective taking and fluid self-to-data relationships in informal open-ended data exploration. *Journal of the learning sciences, 20*(1), 32–56. https://doi.org/10.1080/10508406.2019.1651317

Rubel, L. H., Lim, V. Y., Hall-Wieckert, M., & Sullivan, M. (2016). Teaching mathematics for spatial justice: An investigation of the lottery. *Cognition and Instruction, 34*(1), 1–26. https://doi.org/10.1080/07370008.2015.1118691

Smarr, L. (2012). Quantifying your body: A how-to guide from a systems biology perspective. *Biotechnology Journal, 7*(8), 980–991. https://doi.org/10.1002/biot.201100495

Smith, B., Sharma, P., & Hooper, P. (2006). Decision making in online fantasy sports communities. *Interactive Technology and Smart Education, 3*(4), 347–360. https://doi.org/10.1108/17415650680000072

Tabassum, M., Kosinski, T., & Lipford, H. R. (2019). "I don't own the data": End user perceptions of smart home device data practices and risks. In *Fifteenth Symposium on Usable Privacy and Security (SOUPS 2019)* (pp. 435–450).

Taylor, K., Headrick, & Hall, R. (2013). Counter-mapping the neighborhood on bicycles: Mobilizing youth to reimagine the city. *Technology, Knowledge and Learning, 18*(1–2), 56–93. https://doi.org/10.1007/s10758-013-9201-5

Van Wart, S., Lanouette, K., & Parikh, T. S. (2020). Scripts and counterscripts in community-based data science: Participatory digital mapping and the pursuit of a third space. *Journal of the Learning Sciences, 20*(1), 127–153. https://doi.org/10.1080/10508406.2019.1693378

Wolf, G. (2010). The data-driven life. *New York Times Magazine.* Retrieved from https://www.nytimes.com/2010/05/02/magazine/02self-measurement-t.html?_r=1&ref=magazine

Expansive Views for Data Science Education

6

For many who are enthusiastic about data science, there is the tacit assumption that it is deeply quantitative and computational and those are the most essential areas where people must develop intellectually in order to contribute to the field. Along these lines, it is implied that statistical, mathematical, and computational proficiencies are what matter most for participating in data science. Other areas then, such as studies about society, psychology, and the humanities, feel ancillary. However, among the growing community of K-12 data science educators, there are vocal and justified challenges to this image of data and data science. Parts of this are entangled in larger observations and commentaries about documented harms and risks associated with data science and adjacent fields. For instance, data and algorithmic systems have been used in ways that exclude or oppress groups of people—whether it was the initial deployment of Apple's HealthKit which did not include menstrual cycle tracking despite it being valuable to half of the population (Lewis, 2014) or the ways in which predictive policing systems that tend to have more data on arrests for people of color can lead to a cycle of directing policing to collect and produce more arrest data in those communities even if crime is more uniformly spread out (Shapiro, 2017).

Recognizing that, at present, data science is popularly associated with classical images of mathematical and statistical inquiry that are treated as purely objective, this chapter is intended to more explicitly spotlight that arguments are being put forward that I consider to be more expansive perspectives on data science and data science education. I use the term "expansive" to stress that this is a broadening of scope than what is currently normative. Others may see these as more social, critical, feminist, postmodern, or another descriptor connoting a way of understanding human and social complexity.

DOI: 10.4324/9781003385264-6

These are all noteworthy perspectives on their own and merit careful reads for those interested. At the same time, there are some shared concerns to highlight. While in some communities, this type of work is not seen as part and parcel of data science, I hope that the valuable points that are emerging from expansive perspectives will ultimately be broadly recognized as central to the work of data science and made an essential strand within K-12 data science education. That is, if undergraduate data science degrees and certificates become a form of gatekeeper to professional work (itself a point of concern among some who recognize these opportunities are not available to all), I would hope that expansive views of data science are taken seriously and made a curriculum staple—and in ways that are more than a lone severable course that does not provoke deep critical examination and reflection of data science as a field, set of practices, or ways of knowing.

There are a few intertwined threads that tend to appear in expansive views that I list below. As I discuss some key ideas from specific contributors to expansive perspectives, some of these threads will be revisited.

- **Thread 1: Data are more than numbers and character strings.** One of the most simplified interpretation of this thread is that images, video, locations, and other media are data. This may seem unproblematic for data scientists who could point to the fact that much of professional data are managed as information representations. In hexadecimal, the color red in hex code is #FF0000. Certain image files can be thought of as sets of numbers or vectors specifying details about pixels or image features (relative positions on a 2-D plane and locations of lines in an image, for example). However, the matter at hand from an expansive perspective is not strictly that we have the ability to symbolically represent parts of the world as numbers and character strings, but rather the very decisions to do so and to value that as the preferred information representation should be re-examined and challenged.

- **Thread 2: There are many valid and valuable ways of knowing in data science.** Computational outcomes, whether they are a precise value, interval, or a measure of likelihood, are treated as important ways to draw inferences in data science. However, this is not exhaustive with respect to epistemologies—or how we come to understand things. For instance, stories are an important way to present information and persuade that operate differently than a proof presented using propositional logic.

- **Thread 3: Data and data science are social constructions and thus have associated limits and opportunities.** The measurement systems that we have in place are the product of mutual agreements that have taken a lot of work to establish, but they are social products nonetheless. That we consider it to be 5:00 PM in one location when it is 7:00 PM in another is an agreement made even though the extent of visible daylight and relative temperatures may be different. The technical definition of 1 meter, as established by the International System of Units (SI), is the length of the path of light in vacuum during the time interval of 1/299,792,458th of a second (note: a second has a similar precise definition). This holds true for all other measures, such as standardized test scores, credit ratings, healthiness, or markers of pollution. It is possible for there to be other social constructions for the parts of the world we seek to measure, instead, and these can yield different implications.

- **Thread 4: How we use data science is not neutral, and can lead to harm.** Data science is used to make inferences and help in decision-making, defining groups, and making comparisons. Decisions matter to the extent that different decisions will produce different outcomes, which can have different matrices of costs and benefits. Defining groups creates a social object that becomes part of a larger social system in which distributions can change (e.g., credit scores below 600 will be declined for a loan, luxury vacation packages should be advertised to one income demographic, etc.). Comparisons are a means of recognizing and articulating differences and choosing to consider or ignore those differences that can have differential effects. For example, deciding one student is more desirable for having completed more Advanced Placement® (AP) courses than another but the respective schools have unequal numbers of offerings is a difference that may need to be considered. Deciding some people are more valuable for some reason (such as for a company or insurance payout) because of higher income can be an alarming way to make an appraisal of human importance.

- **Thread 5. Humans and communities must have agency regarding data and data science.** Because of whatever accumulated historical and ideological forces are in play, there are places where the production and use of data are viewed very differently. In some places, government surveillance using sophisticated data science (and likely artificial intelligence) would be deemed very acceptable, necessary for safety and smooth operations, and not something to challenge. In others, that would be absolutely unacceptable and grounds for protest and legislative action. Similarly, the idea that data belong to different entities or can be shared with different levels of permission is another way in which agency is viewed in complex ways. The expansive perspective tends to recognize that in places like the United States, current infrastructures and norms enable specific enterprise entities to produce and procure data for their use and gain. Many are pushing for more transparency and individual choice about data given that the benefits and harms of its use may distribute in ways counter to what an individual wants.

Having stated these threads first, I now turn to describing some key ideas from the data science education research literatures that contribute to expansive perspectives for data science education.

A Humanistic Stance

I have collaborated with my respected colleagues Michelle Wilkerson and Kathryn Lanouette to put forward a call for data science education to be more humanistic in its approach (Lee et al., 2021). By humanistic, we mean an acknowledgment that data science education operates and contributes to a complex human-constructed world. One way that we suggested seeing this is by attending to layers of mediation in data science. Stated more simply, when we learn about and do things with data, there are social touch points that may go unrecognized but are there. For example, inviting students to work with sensor data in science class could look like: (1) Having each students use off-the-shelf sensor technologies to generate information to store online. (2) Having each student use a microcontroller board like the micro:bit and program their own sensors to collect data. (3) Having students share sensors and record measurements on individual lab books. (4) Using a downloadable file from a sensor network or website that provides data sets to teachers.

Can we recognize some of the implications of these four different approaches? Will all four configurations have the same expectations and proficiencies for what it means to work with sensor data in professional science? Will the understanding of the things being measured be the same if students are not collecting the data firsthand by themselves (Hug & McNeill, 2008)? Are all of these available and accessible to all students and classrooms or dependent on other factors such as budgets, online platform compatibility? If this were sensing water quality, how does the meaning and importance of this activity differ for students in a rural agricultural community or students in a city with neglected water infrastructure?

Clearly, there can be a lot of things to consider, and my colleagues and I put forward three layers to attend to when adopting a humanistic stance. One is personal—how data and the individual experiences can be intertwined; one is cultural—how do different tools, norms, and ways of doing things manifest in the data experience; one is sociopolitical—how a data experience and the subsequent learning fits into a world where the meanings and uses of data are part of how power and influence are negotiated both immediately and in distant ways.

In several ways, versions of this play out in current debates about data science education. For example, if students aren't learning programming (a set of cultural tools), are they actually employable for high-paying jobs with well-known companies that have societal influence (a sociopolitical concern)? If students only learn how data science has been used harmfully, will there ever be the ability to foster appreciation (a personal piece) for interesting and helpful contributions that data science could help facilitate? The opposite view could be taken and has been voiced by critics of data science—if students maintain the status quo in their data science educational experiences, are they reinforcing current structures and systems and making it harder to challenge those? Will access and opportunity be available to all if things are not changed?

Felt Data

In their study of division 1 college athletes, Clegg and colleagues (2023) observed athletes attending to "felt data"—what their bodies told them implicitly about their performance. For example, they describe athletes using felt data ("felt my hamstrings firing") as support for where they felt they needed to direct their strength training when arguing in favor of the coach shifting training focus to hamstrings. This became for many athletes a kind of recognition of what is referenced with certain quantifications. Indeed, in exercise science, there are ideas about perceived exertion that are quantified but also expressed in qualitative metrics (e.g., can hold a conversation at a specific level of intensity). This is something that gives an indexical relationship from body sensation to numerical records—an almost reverse configuration of how we tend to see data as a representation of some object or experience in the world.

I mention this because I have seen felt data in my own research. In a study of endurance runners and cyclists (Lee & Drake, 2013), cyclists talked about how they could feel what 85 rpms (a common target) felt like and did not need to look to their sensor equipment to make the next decision or evaluate their performance. One participant in general found the alignment of her own subjective feeling of exhaustion and what was the corresponding heart rate on her heart rate monitor to be enlightening and validating. As she described seeing that her feelings of exhaustion corresponded to a heart rate above 200 beats per minute,

I need to, I need to walk through this. This is absolutely ridiculous to have it be that high… That's why I have such a strong desire to walk. Because my body is saying, "You've got to slow down, you've got to let that heart rate drop." And all of a sudden, it was, *"I'm not a wimp. I'm pretty tough if I can get it to that high."*

Stacy (an interviewee in Lee & Drake, 2013, excerpted from that article, p. 59, emphasis in original)

Similarly, in research on families helping children manage the data work around type 1 diabetes (Lee & Dubovi, 2020), one family had created a novel system at home to work on numeracy and how to think about different categories of glucose readings for their son who had not yet begun schooling. The desired range of values, where they placed a marker together as a family in order to jointly practice interpreting the glucometer reading, was on paper that was colored white. The son was asked to notice how his body felt then and when in other color zones on their large number line. They developed a slogan for him "white feels right". In this example, the bodily feeling and active recognition and acknowledgment were important (Figure 6.1).

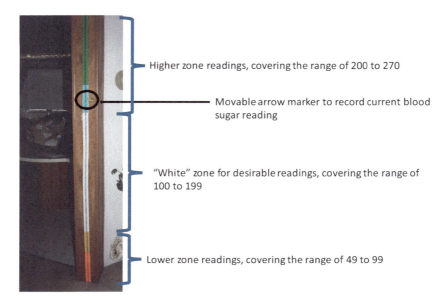

Figure 6.1 One family's door frame system to show different numerical values of blood sugar to help their type 1 diabetic child get more familiar with different readings and how to think about them in relation to one another.

But is this something that we ought to consider as data? Some may challenge that, but an expansive view would consider this permissible. One might ask, what are data if there is no referent for the quantification or the label? Therefore, the referent (in this case, the sensation or experience) is part of the entire thing we understand as data. Alternately, another way of thinking about the validity of felt data is to consider that even the subjective bodily sensations are an abstraction from something larger. In the case of some physical fitness, it is one small noted facet of a larger experience that can also involve objects (weights, a ball, other players) and other important features (decision and intention to pursue some level of exertion, the product of years of training to enable a specific feeling to exist at a certain level of performance, etc.). Again, these may be raised as questions for more narrowed views of data, but be seen as expansive and important—particularly for learning that centralizes data and the operation of the human body.

Small Data

With all the attention directed to "big data", particularly among enthusiasts of analytics and data that are being continuously generated at a massive scale, some researchers have also advanced an idea of small data. Calabrese Barton et al. (2021) characterize small data as including "daily life experiences, perspectives, stories, and family/community histories as worthy data to grapple with" (p. 2). In their study of critical data practices among youth in the midst of the COVID-19 pandemic when they were actively reconciling large amounts of information and data about what was happening and what groups of people were being differentially affected, they noted that small data were important to recognize especially for those individuals and groups who are marginalized and have limited digital footprints. In one sense, big data didn't exist for some groups. In the sense that data direct attention, resources, and power, it is necessary to recognize that data that are not "big" in the big data sense have importance and also direct attention, resources, and power.

Considering small data with a critical eye, a major concern is in data's influence and recognition of importance as a source of information and backing for an argument. The key properties of data that are small data are not necessarily that they exist in numerical form or conform to tidy structures or are even plural (a small datum maybe?). Rather, the key properties are its power-laden force and functional purpose as what we consider to be (small) data can provide good backing or justification.

Rubel et al. (2016) juxtaposed small data, albeit not using that exact terminology, in youth data investigations about the presence and promotion of lottery ticket sales in lower income neighborhoods, typically those occupied by people of color. As part of their work, the youth gained deeper understandings of maps, spatial justice, and communities along with data that they had recorded. Among the data that were validated and included in this work was interviews with community members, photographs, and other records. Similar endeavors had been undertaken in van Wart et al. (2020).

Often, the work reporting on and arguing in favor of recognition of small data comes from adept qualitative researchers. Qualitative research, often drawing on observations, interviews, artifacts, and experiences, has a robust (but shared) presence in education research, as well as other academic fields. High-quality qualitative research is conducted with rigor and does require the gathering and analysis of data, albeit those data are not in numerical forms nor subject to the same computational techniques that operate on numerical information. These are indeed data that must be carefully obtained and processed in this mode of research, and they serve as empirical support. Debates on the utility and value of different research paradigms have been and are still ongoing, although there is, in general, an agreement in education that multiple paradigms and techniques have their place in the work and contribute to scientific understandings (Shavelson & Towne, 2002).

An objection to small data is that it is a different thing entirely than big data, and it is the ability to work with big data that is the concern of data science. However, I believe that the advocacy of small data from an expansive perspective is to intentionally challenge that perception, with an awareness that what is recognized as important tends to be that which gets called "big data", even though there is "data science" in the small data as well, and it must receive attention too as we turn more to data with the push for data science.

Images, Video, and Other Media as Data

Already alluded to in earlier sections (see Digital Media section of Chapter 5), an expansive perspective maintains appreciation of objects such as photographs, video interviews, social media short form videos, written journals, and other artifacts as data. As stated in the beginning of this chapter, it is not in the sense that these can be represented in a form that computers can manipulate. Rather, these are records of experience and are key to our actions and interpretations. Like the sections above, this is a challenge to viewing data as structured numbers, labels, and characters.

These other media can be quite compelling and serve as evidence. In history, there are a number of classic images that become part of collective memory, whether in the United States it was of the moon landing or the photograph of Kim Phúc running naked following a napalm attack in South Vietnam. These are the records of critical events and are not ones that we can simply go back and collect more. The importance of these is understood and reiterated in their description and invocation. In court cases, video and photographs can be important records for drawing conclusions.

Before the push for statistics, or even written records, would we believe there to be no data in existence? Specimens and objects are central to a lot of our theories and models of the past. Field notes are still important for biology. There are ways of interpreting these items that do not lend themselves to arithmetical operations.

The most conservative treatment of these as images and other forms of data could be they are an adjunct and limited form. However, expansive treatments would see these as valuable in their own right. Furthermore, these are compelling and meaningful to people outside of a formal learning context. It would be appropriate to acknowledge and draw upon them, even if there are some practices and ways of thinking we also wish to foster through mathematical, statistical, and computational methods as well.

Data Feminism

In 2020, D'Ignazio and Klein published a book that is available for purchase in bound format and free to read online titled *Data Feminism*. Data feminism is defined as "a way of thinking about data, both their uses and their limits, that is informed by direct experience, by a commitment to action, and by intersectional feminist thought" (p. 8), and the book was intentionally written for data scientist audiences. Feminist activism and thought has named ways in which sexism persists in society and spoken on in the pursuit of equitable futures. There are many approaches, some of which align directly with the term "feminism" and some that intentionally distance themselves so as to highlight other aspects (such as other axes of inequality, such as race or sexual orientation). The authors acknowledge the range of these uses, and make clear how they use the term.

As has been demonstrated numerous times, existing social systems and power structures that have persisted over time have overlooked, erased, or selectively represented the contributions of specific individuals and groups of people over time to important lines of thought. For example, as MacArthur winning author Alison Bechdel (1986) has humorously observed in one of her published comics, there is an easy way to see how women have been poorly and underrepresented in popular film. The Bechdel test to show this is quite simple, and it involves a film having three components:

1. The film stars a woman
2. Who talks to another woman
3. About something other than a man

It can be humbling to recognize how many lauded films that have been decorated with awards over time cannot pass this test, either because there is only one speaking woman in the film or because the women are never talking to one another or as something that exists in relation to being supports for or objects of desire for men. In the summer of 2023, the film *Barbie* was an example where the test had been passed, and critics found it to be a thoughtful commentary on sexism as well as entertaining with great visuals, jokes, and pacing.

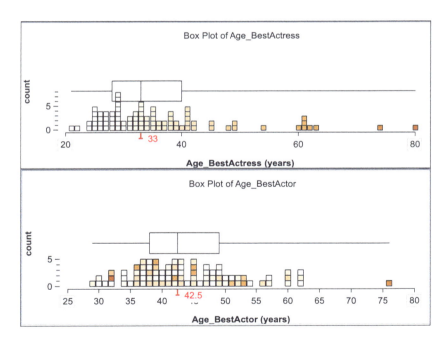

Figure 6.2 Box plots of Oscar Best Actor and Best Actress ages at time of award, rendered in *TinkerPlots*.

Data can be a tool for making visible these inequities. The Geena Davis Institute on Gender and Media has released reports (e.g., 2015) and data showing discrepancies in speaking time for different gender characters. The average age of best actor and best actress recipients at the Academy awards has some alarming patterns as well (see Figure 6.2). One, although far from the only point of data feminism, is that data can be a way to make visible inequalities and how power manifests itself in a range of activities and situations. For instance, in her study of information systems and search engines, MacArthur award winning information scientist Safiya Noble (2018) showed how search engine results will yield images reflecting negative stereotypes for Black Girls compared to White Girls, among many other alarming results. This is a product of a longstanding pattern of unequal participation in internet content production and labeling as well as a lack of attention from companies and engineers to these social and cultural forces.

Data Feminism is rich with examples and arguments about how data science is being discussed and recognized in society and it is one read that I would recommend to anyone interested in data science. In addition to examples and strong arguments, D'Ignazio and Klein identify seven principles informed by and part of data feminism. These are:

1. Examine Power
2. Challenge Power
3. Elevate Emotion & Embodiment
4. Rethink Binaries & Hierarchies
5. Embrace Pluralism
6. Consider Context
7. Make Labor Visible

Beyond showing injustices and oppression with data, the authors invite feminist epistemologies that leading philosophers and psychologists have advanced in other lines of work (e.g., Gilligan, 1993). This includes ways of reasoning that respect the importance of thinking relationally or considering the virtue of care to be one of importance tremendous importance when we operate in a world that tends to value abstractions, images of objectivity, and specific logic structures.

In one collaboration, I was part of a group that looked at where a number of data science education efforts in the academic literature for K-12 stood in relation to the principles of data feminism (Lee et al., 2022). Given the increased attention and slower pace of academic publishing, there is probably more to say now than what we could say then. Objections to data feminism tend to be of the sort that are precisely what data feminism objects to. Narrowing the inclusion of what is valued in data science to be numbers, computation, and big data so as to bring about some order of things in the world are precisely the values that data feminism seeks to interrogate. There could be some critiques raised that despite its push for greater egalitarianism, there is still limited representation of many groups in what is recognized as feminism. There are also misunderstandings. However, these are hopefully things that can be corrected over time through greater awareness and inclusion efforts.

Data Sovereignty

In the introductory chapter, I mentioned how in the rush to pursue new commercial opportunities, "data is the new oil" with its complicated implications (e.g., Hirsch, 2014). The collection of data, especially through online activity and use of platforms that appear to be "free" for use, are often ways for companies and other organizations to accrue data that can then be used to modify products and offerings in service of further growth. Some groups sell or share these data to partners. In the fine print of privacy policies at the time that someone signs up for an online service or platform, these activities are stated in buried and complicated text. It is in the company's or organization's interest to have control over these data.

The push toward data sovereignty challenges this pattern. On the one hand, this becomes a question about privacy and individual liberties. In Europe, the GDPR (General Data Protection Regulation) treats data as the property of the individual and that the individual maintains fundamental rights regarding the collection and use of those data. Given the large number of people using online systems, GDPR has had a major effect on how many apps and systems operate, else they would not be in compliance for the European Union.

Beyond that, there are ways in which data gathering and use has been extractive and used in ways that have been considered exploitative. Some communities have long histories of mistreatment. A push toward data sovereignty is one for the communities from which data are generated or about whom the data refer and belong to and are for the use (and benefit) of those communities. For example, Indigenous communities and nations have suffered atrocities that came about from colonialism and decades of policies from governments that established themselves on Indigenous land (see Hansen et al., 2024, for a curriculum project to surface this). For data about an Indigenous community, who should have the ultimate say on what data are collected, of whom, and for what purpose? Data sovereignty principles would be clear that the Indigenous communities should have the full decision-making power (Kukutai & Taylor, 2016; Walter et al., 2021). The reasons are many, but at a minimum, to end cycles of exploitation and to allow communities to empower themselves with data are among those. Additionally, data as social constructions can produce and perpetuate ways of thinking and stereotypes that may be counter to and harmful to groups of people who may elect to understand things differently and find their own favored ways to be more productive for their own needs.

Objections to data sovereignty may be that innovation and competitiveness rely on data, and, over time, benefits for different groups of people are realized by virtue of the market systems that are in place. However, these are precisely some of the principles that are challenged. To date, there is still more to be reconciled regarding data sovereignty, and, as far as data science in K-12 goes, they may be better approached and understood if this is included and centered as part of what we learn and contend with in K-12 data science education.

Keeping an Eye on a Larger, Growing Body of Work

This chapter barely scratches the surface of a set of challenging issues for data science, the systems in which data science is embedded, and in how we organize and design education for data science. It is very appropriate that this is a matter for K-12 data science education and its affiliated research communities. K-12 education is thought to serve a number of purposes, but among those are beliefs about opportunity, social mobility, and helping equip the next generation to imagine and build the world that they will continue to steward in the future. Education research and practice also attracts a multitude of perspectives as we all need methodological and intellectual hands on deck for understanding and helping the further improvement of this very complex set of institutions and practices.

Because this chapter scratches the surface, it is largely meant to be a pointer to some, and only some, of the notable ideas that are expanding how we view and educate about data science. This has contact with critical examinations of technology in society that show more examples that centrally involve data but may be seen as heavily tied to specific technologies where the role of data work is not always as obvious on the surface. Work to examine includes but is not limited to that of Buolamwini and Gebru (2018), Noble (2018), Benjamin (2019), and O'Neil (2016)—some of whom are mentioned earlier in some of the earlier text of this chapters or elsewhere in this book. Tofel-Grehl and

Schanzer (2024) have also released an edited collection in a book from which several cited works in this book appear, about issues of equity across K-16 data science education. As much work still remains to be done, we should expect more works to help further refine key ideas emerging in expansive views that contribute to and ultimately move closer to centrality in data science education.

References

Bechdel, A. (1986). *Dykes to watch out for*. Ithaca, NY: Firebrand Books

Benjamin, R. (2019). *Race after technology: Abolitionist tools for the new Jim Code*. New York: Polity Books.

Buolamwini, J., & Gebru, T. (2018). *Gender shades: Intersectional accuracy disparities in commercial gender classification*. Paper presented at the Proceedings of the 1st Conference on Fairness, Accountability and Transparency, Proceedings of Machine Learning Research. Retrieved from https://proceedings.mlr.press/v81/buolamwini18a.html

Calabrese Barton, A., Greenberg, D., Turner, C., Riter, D., Perez, M., Tasker, T., … Davis, E. A. (2021). Youth critical data practices in the COVID-19 multipandemic. *AERA Open, 7*, 23328584211041631. https://doi.org/10.1177/23328584211041631

Clegg, T. L., Cleveland, K., Weight, E., Greene, D., & Elmqvist, N. (2023). Data everyday as community-driven science: Athletes' critical data literacy practices in collegiate sports contexts. *Journal of Research in Science Teaching, 60*(8), 1786–1816. https://doi.org/10.1002/tea.21842

D'Ignazio, C., & Klein, L. F. (2020). *Data feminism*. Cambridge: MIT Press.

Geena Davis Institute on Gender in Media. (2015). *The reel truth: Women aren't seen or heard*. Retrieved from https://geenadavisinstitute.org/research/the-reel-truth-women-arent-seen-or-heard/

Gilligan, C. (1993). *In a different voice: Psychological theory and women's development*. Cambridge, MA: Harvard University Press.

Hansen, T., Searle, K., Jiang, M., & Barker, M. (2024). Shrinking lands and growing perspectives: Affordances of data science literacy during a culturally responsive maker project. In C. Tofel-Grehl & E. Schanzer (Eds.), *Improving equity in data science* (pp. 37–56). New York, NY: Routledge.

Hirsch, D. D. (2014). The glass house effect: Big data, the new oil, and the power of analogy. *Maine Law Review, 66*(2), 373.

Hug, B., & McNeill, K. L. (2008). Use of First-hand and Second-hand data in science: Does data type influence classroom conversations? *International Journal of Science Education, 30*(13), 1725–1751.

Kukutai, T., & Taylor, J. (2016). *Indigenous data sovereignty: Toward an agenda*. Canberra: ANU Press.

Lee, V. R., & Drake, J. (2013). Digital physical activity data collection and use by endurance runners and distance cyclists. *Technology, Knowledge and Learning, 18*(1–2), 39–63. https://doi.org/10.1007/s10758-013-9203-3

Lee, V. R., & Dubovi, I. (2020). At home with data: Family engagements with data involved in Type 1 Diabetes management. *Journal of the Learning Sciences, 20*(1), 11–31. https://doi.org/10.1080/10508406.2019.1666011

Lee, V. R., Pimentel, D. R., Bhargava, R., & D'Ignazio, C. (2022). Taking data feminism to school: A synthesis and review of pre-collegiate data science education projects. *British Journal of Educational Technology, 55*(3), 1096–1113. https://doi.org/10.1111/bjet.13251

Lee, V. R., Wilkerson, M. H., & Lanouette, K. (2021). A call for a humanistic stance toward K-12 data science education. *Educational Researcher, 50*(9), 664–672. https://doi.org/10.3102/0013189X211048810

Lewis, T. (2014). Apple's health app tracks almost everything, except periods. *NBC News*. Retrieved from https://www.nbcnews.com/id/wbna56126216

Noble, S. (2018). *Algorithms of oppression: How search engines reinforce racism*. New York, NY: New York University Press.

O'Neil, C. (2016). *Weapons of math destruction: How big data increases inequality and threatens democracy*. New York, NY: Broadway Books.

Rubel, L. H., Lim, V. Y., Hall-Wieckert, M., & Sullivan, M. (2016). Teaching mathematics for spatial justice: An investigation of the lottery. *Cognition and Instruction, 34*(1), 1–26. https://doi.org/10.1080/07370008.2015.1118691

Shapiro, A. (2017). Reform predictive policing. *Nature, 541*(7638), 458–460. https://doi.org/10.1038/541458a

Shavelson, R. J., & Towne, L. (Eds.). (2002). *Scientific research in education*. Washington, DC: National Academy Press.

Tofel-Grehl, C., & Schanzer, E. (2024). *Improving equity in data science: Re-imagining the teaching and learning of data in K-16 Classrooms*. New York: Taylor & Francis.

Van Wart, S., Lanouette, K., & Parikh, T. S. (2020). Scripts and counterscripts in community-based data science: Participatory digital mapping and the pursuit of a third space. *Journal of the Learning Sciences, 20*(1), 127–153. https://doi.org/10.1080/10508406.2019.1693378

Walter, M., Lovett, R., Maher, B., Williamson, B., Prehn, J., Bodkin-Andrews, G., & Lee, V. (2021). Indigenous data sovereignty in the era of big data and open data. *Australian Journal of Social Issues, 56*(2), 143–156. https://doi.org/10.1002/ajs4.141

Onward—A Data Science Education Research Ecosystem 7

Although data have been part of educational standards for mathematics, science, computer science, and even social studies for quite some time already, we seem to be in the early stages of a concerted push and adoption of data science education in K-12. As we look toward the future, what are things we ought to keep in mind—beyond the research that already exists? Are there ways in which this can be more than a flash in the pan and part of a sustained commitment to strengthening data skills in ways that create opportunities for richer participation in data conversations and ways that exercise appropriate caution? The goal of this chapter is to reflect on that and consider some of the larger systemic needs as they stand currently. It is not explicitly policy guidance nor is it about systems change. Rather, it takes into consideration some of the more recent conversations in the field, some synthesis efforts from the last decade, and thoughts on how we might position ourselves for a sustained future for data science in K-12.

The Challenge of Rapidly Changing Technological Possibilities

Mathematics and Reading are considered mainstays of K-12 instruction, and their status as essential to the school experience is reinforced by state and international comparative testing. While I am familiar with some things related to assessment design and use, I am not an expert on testing policy. However, as both a parent and an education researcher who collaborates with

DOI: 10.4324/9781003385264-7

classrooms and schools regularly, it is evident from conversations with teachers, principals, parents, and research colleagues that testing still maintains an iron-claw grip on what we deem essential in the education system. This is something that will take a lot of time to change, if it even does ultimately change. Regardless, the focus on testing creates mandatory commitments and priorities for schools and classrooms. This has ways in which it can be beneficial and ways in which it can create challenges.

At the same time, there is a sense that the world is changing. To be fair, the world is always changing. But some visible changes are ones that are part and parcel with advances in and large-scale appropriation of technology. In my own K-12 schooling, well-resourced schools had perhaps a couple of computers (Apple IIes often) in the back of the classroom. The internet was only something for universities and not well-known in the public. Even modems were not widely known technology (they may not be all that widely known now, as a reflection of how change is not necessarily cumulative).

There had been pioneering efforts among researchers to do interesting work with computers in schools. Some of it involved creating pathways for students to do programming (e.g., Papert, 1980), some with tutoring systems (Anderson et al., 1995); others involved using advanced tools that scientists were beginning to use such as visualizations (Gomez et al., 1998); some looked at networked modifiable knowledge repositories (Scardamalia & Bereiter, 2006); some involved scaffolded web-based curriculum (Linn & Hsi, 2000); and some even went toward laser discs for instruction that was anchored in stories and contexts (Cognition & Technology Group at Vanderbilt, 1990). Some excellent summaries of the histories leading to work in this vein can be found in Pea and Linn (2020), and I will disclose that as someone trained in and deeply involved in the field of Learning Sciences, the examples that come to mind most immediately are partial and skew toward ones that are canonized in our research communities.

The internet became more widely available with more schools getting connectivity, and the public turned more to the internet for activities like websurfing and a little bit of e-commerce. Handheld technologies were an interesting way of exploring mobility and computing that could be with individual students (Roschelle & Pea, 2002; Soloway et al., 2001), and cell phones began to transition from unusual items to have to becoming increasingly pervasive. Internet search improved and people shared media (sometimes in violation of copyright laws) with one another. Search engines became more impressive at helping users find information they wanted. Apple released the first iPhone in 2007, and the touch screen interface and greater internet connectivity on the go became more commonplace.

Throughout this time, there were visions of computer-based curriculum and computers that were abundant and readily used by schools. (This is an appropriate time to, of course, mention Larry Cuban's work documented in *Oversold and Underused* (2001). Purchasing and providing the technology to schools by itself does not lead to meaningful use in schools. Similarly, hype and just providing relatively inexpensive but high-potential technology does not speak to larger complex challenges that can be missed—see Ames (2019)). Some push continued for computer courses which tended to focus on basic computer literacy, productivity software usage, search, and internet use. For a while, it felt like 1980s, 1990s, and 2000s were gradual progressions in education and its role in preparing people for a world with technology. There were, of course, more ambitious calls and visions being made but they were not part of the larger educational mainstream beyond researchers and some educators (diSessa, 2000).

However, coinciding with the rise of big tech companies, we are seeing new ways that technology is integrating into work and life. More computing devices were appearing in more places, and while many forces were at work, mobile devices launched an explosion of more people interested in developing phone apps. While Pets.com stumbled and failed in the late 90s, Chewy.com became mainstream in the 2010s and 2020s—both being forward-thinking pet food and pet supply internet delivery services—an example that I mention to make the point that things changed with respect to how the public, at least in the United States, was responding differently to online services and interactions as times and infrastructures changed. Jeannette Wing (2006) issued a call for teaching computational thinking, the Maker movement (summarized historically in Blikstein, 2018) excited the public about everyday people building with digital tools, and a new vision for libraries as media authoring spaces was being put forward (Austin et al., 2011). While the story is more complex than that, the idea of computer science as a subject for all students to encounter in some form advanced more computer coding in schools. That has been a new addition into the curriculum (that still is needing work and support, despite its growth in the past decade). In some efforts, it is more computer science courses and pathways for students, including new computer science curricula for schools, integrating computer science with other subject areas (what had been from the National Science Foundation referred to as STEM+C to pursue ways of teaching science, technology, engineering, or mathematics with computer science), more computer science and programming-oriented toys and products being purchased for schools, and free online programming environments that used block-based programming and emphasized the creation of games and animations. The Maker movement inspired schools to create makerspaces and purchase 3-D printers and seek ways to use them as part of classroom instruction, so teaching digital fabrication or using it in instruction became a thing.

Still new technology developments took off further. Cybersecurity became a more pressing concern and received funding attention. It led to the launch of new projects. Social media was contributing to cyberbullying and misinformation, and so a push toward digital citizenship and to teaching more media literacy came about. Cloud computing has become more pervasive, and some schools started to team with Amazon to teach Amazon Web Services (AWS). Blockchain, especially as used in cryptocurrency, had a quick heyday and even momentarily became a popular topic of technological interest. Data science garnered attention as universities and industry were forming programs, job titles, and visible public figures. But then we have suddenly become struck with generative artificial intelligence (AI) capabilities and a push is under way for teaching AI in schools. More may come down the pipeline, perhaps biocomputing or quantum computing or a push for autonomous robotics or bioinformatics. These are indeed interesting areas of innovation and research, but will they be accompanied by a push to have these be part of classroom instruction?

This is where things are starting to get untenable. At the current moment, these new developments tend to inspire some individuals to ask the question "What if we could have kids learn this cool new stuff too?", and depending on how much political savvy and attention certain advocates can muster, this may move into the classroom. Will education and education research keep jumping from one hot technology topic to another, make a push for some part of the K-12 education to cover it, and then move on to the next shiny new topic?

This is a question that the National Academies of Science, Engineering, and Medicine (NASEM) is currently considering. Likely, by the time this book is out, a consensus report from the academies will already be released. NASEM has put forward that much of what we are seeing now with the jump from one new technology development to another in society is relying heavily on some combination of data and computing. Therefore, rather than new efforts springing up for each new societal technology development, we should ask what are the core competences that underlie these new directions, many of which have yet to even come into being. I agree this is a good premise to have.[1]

Bringing the focus to data science education and the current pattern of new calls for new topics of instruction in schools, my rhetorical goal is to make apparent that this is happening, it seems to be happening faster than before, and in light of this being the prevailing tendency right now with new technologies in the world that we should think about whether data science education is one trend or there is some sort of staying power. The fact that this book exists suggests a belief that there is some staying power to data science as an area of concern for schools and students. However, I will concede that the name may change—especially given the ways in which data literacy and data science have been pitted against each other (see Chapters 1 and 2), that the push for data science education effectively captured a spotlight that did not seem to be there for K-12 statistics education, and that there are ways we can imagine it being folded into other topics such as machine learning education, computer science education, a new vision of mathematics education or science education, or even AI literacy education. But in some manner, taking into consideration the magnitudes of data that have been produced and stored digitally and are continuing to be produced and stored digitally and that we can see how work with data is consequential to many new technologies (e.g., generative AI and machine learning both rely on data to do the impressive things that they can do), I expect K-12 data science education—in some form—will stay in the spotlight for quite a while. Assuming it is going to become part of the fabric of K-12 schooling, we will need to consider how it fits into a very full curriculum (Jiang et al., 2022). That is already a contentious topic, as the renewed debates about mathematics teaching and necessary courses for students in California have illustrated.

Maintaining Visibility

Important to keeping data science education in view is ensuring it remains visible and part of our conversations about education. While this has been a concerted effort involving many people in many parts of the world for quite some time, it is worth noting that an important moment of public visibility came from Steven Leavitt's *Freakonomics* podcast released on October 2, 2019, titled "America's Math Curriculum Doesn't Add Up". Throughout the podcast, Leavitt discusses helping his teenaged children with their mathematics homework and finds that the things they are learning have little applicability to things he sees as more common in daily life.

> I believe that we owe it to our children to prepare them for the world that they will encounter—a world driven by data. Basic data fluency is a requirement not just for most good jobs, but also for navigating life more generally. Whether it is in terms of financial literacy, making good choices about our own health, or knowing who and what to

believe. Math class isn't the only place to teach data skills, but it seems like a good place to start.

(From the Freakonomics Podcast, Oct. 2, 2019)

I share this because not long after this podcast came out, a consortium operating out of University of Chicago (where Levitt is a professor) called Data Science 4 Everyone (DS4E) (datascience4everyone.org) formed. I have watched their formation and growth and have been pleased with the work there to help make data science in K-12 a real possibility. DS4E has secured funding from major philanthropies, convened experts in the field, held online panels and discussions, formed workgroups, promoted the sharing of data science classroom lessons, talked to state and federal leaders, and been a tremendous advocate for K-12 data science education. They have quickly become a highly visible presence and bridge builder for the field.

One of the bridges they have formed is with the Concord Consortium, an educational research and development nonprofit that developed and maintains the Common Online Data Analysis Platform (CODAP) platform (see Chapter 4) and has been part of numerous projects in service of data science education for many years—even prior to the launch of DS4E. Together, these two groups have organized the inaugural data science education K-12 conference to be held in 2025—a formidable undertaking. There have been intensive efforts to lend their support to national, state, and practitioner organizations and to enlist top individuals from around the country as partners and community members.

However, other forms of visibility are needed. News features, often with data science education as taught with the *Introduction to Data Science* curriculum (Gould et al., 2018), have appeared on television and on the web. The resurrected California Math Wars have led to some op-eds and positions that certainly brought attention to K-12 data science education (see Chapters 1 and 2). Professional organizations, such as the National Council of Teachers of Mathematics (2024) have even issued statements. Individuals with large reach among teachers, including my university colleague Jo Boaler who is widely known among math teachers, have used her platforms to ensure that awareness grows and to point teachers to resources.

What else could or should be done? We will need, among other things, new images of data science education at work in schools, direct testimonies—both formal and informal ones—of the experiences from students and teachers, more systematic empirical research to understand under what configurations it can support student success, public advocates, curriculum development and distribution, and the time and space to teach data science in its appropriate K-12 form well. Something like standards and guides for how to orient toward data science and do so in a way that is feasible and responsive to the realities of school could be helpful too. That could become something for states and districts to use as a reference point as they craft the learning goals that they pursue. This will likely also require serious work on new assessments as the goals are better articulated.

Research Funding and New Innovation

I am a proponent of research funding. Not only is this because I work in research. Research is valuable because not only can new ideas generated from research have immediate practical use (such as for vaccine technology), but also because it can serve as a source of inspiration (such as discoveries of biological mechanisms of action that could inform engineering), or simply foster appreciation of the amazing world in which we live (such as helping us recognize the sheer diversity of species in different environments under different circumstances). Education research, as a social science, occupies an interesting role. On the one hand, there is an immediate desire for actionable findings from that research. On the other hand, education is quite complex and in continual states of change. There is so much we do not understand and many points about education and current systems on which we do not agree. And to add to this, it is often politicized and reduced to headlines when they are much messier when one really understands what the inquiry, argument, and conclusions were. But we could look to education research for charting courses of action for societal improvement, for providing inspiration, and for helping us appreciate what humans are able to do.

For data science education, research seems important if this growing field is going to be an ongoing direction for investment, policy, and practice. This book is intended to establish that there are some things that we have come to understand from areas such as cognitive psychology, statistics education, learning sciences, and other fields. We should remain open, however, that the established lines of inquiry that have been pursued and the associated findings and recommendations may only represent one possible way to pursue data science education given that the landscape of data science practice is changing rapidly especially as technological impacts and presence in society change rapidly (see above). At the time of much foundational statistics education research that informs today's work, there had not been as much progress in thinking about how young people engage in computer programming. Interests and concerns in the world have changed, so what seemed relevant or pertinent to young people have likely also changed. Background knowledge upon which new knowledge is built changes as well. The idea that young people might hear the term "data" and associate with part of mobile phone service plans (Bowler et al., 2017) or how complex students' views can be on what role businesses play for data privacy (Agesilaou & Kyza, 2022) would not have been as prominent or consequential when key statistics education studies were done in the early 1990s. Earlier ideas that had been treated as foundational will need to be updated, and new studies should be welcome.

However, we are at a time when trust and investment in science could be much stronger. What does data science education research look like? It would involve studies of how people think about and understand data science ideas and what facilitates uptake of data science practices. It would involve research into ways that data science is made accessible and is positively changed by new approaches and new groups of people who are participating in it. It would help us to understand questions about developmental appropriateness and take into account that many existing developmental assumptions merit revisiting. Also, it would involve iterative design and refinement of new tools and learning experiences. It is incredibly common for me to be approached by a motivated outsider asking for research on their product to show that "it works", or that "it works better than something else". While that can be a fine area of research, it's narrow and not representative of what knowledge we ultimately seek to develop through research. We need better understandings of why things work, under what conditions, for whom, what is the space of possible alternatives, and what we must continue to understand better. As it stands currently, and perhaps ironically, there is not a lot of quantitative, experimental research on data science education relative to other research approaches. Those types of studies will have greater value when we can determine what path we wish to pursue and as part of larger, fluid conversations about ideas from the field as it grows.

There have been some philanthropic investments that have helped move data science education along, and those are appreciated and ideally something in line with the mission of the philanthropy and its founders. There are compelling ideas coming from many different places, and more mechanisms to solicit those—seed grants for interesting ideas that may or may not take root—are important for a data science education research ecosystem. This does not mean that projects to refine, scale, and evaluate things we believe already work are unworthy of investment—but balance to keep new ideas flowing, with the expectation that some high-risk and some idiosyncratic approaches do a lot for innovation. We need a mix of safe bets for research investment and continuous creation of new possible bets to make.

Also, my push for supporting new ideas does not mean that we should not take stock and synthesize ideas that are building a strong body of evidence. A bad outcome would be to continuously recreate new versions of the same idea and not move the field forward with funded work to articulate what is already known and what is the state of the field. There may be some design processes and principles, robust challenges or consistently reliable strategies, or well-understood mechanisms to state (and of course, periodically update). For instance, a good amount of support for the need to help students think about aggregate properties of data—such as distribution and variation—is needed, challenging, and potentially important for future progress in moving fluidly between thinking about individual cases in data and thinking about what large amounts of data are saying and when either or both are important to consider.

Recent Synthesis Documents

This book's goal is to help keep the ball rolling as data science education in K-12 grows as an area of research, exploration, and innovation. An underlying message of this book is that there has been important work done by others upon which we can and should build. There is a good chance that this list is incomplete, and other resources will surely appear over time. However, good research typically looks toward multiple sources and points of view to support arguments and invite others to push our collective understanding forward. With that in mind, here are some books or reports that seem timely and helpful for research.

NASEM has been an important player in education research in that it launches studies to report on the state of the field for some topic. This has the power of shifting attention and conversations in important ways, and they have a high bar for who is appointed to committees, transparency, what can and cannot be said on the basis of available evidence, and vetting of report drafts by anonymous experts. There are reports that touch on data and data science as it interacts with science instruction that are mostly recognized as reports for the science education or math education community. The focus here is on those that speak to data science and education specifically.

For undergraduate education, a major report released in 2018 provided recommendations for postsecondary instruction. The report was informed by expert reviews of some of the earliest formal undergraduate programs in data science, specific courses and minors about data offered in undergraduate institutions, the activities taking place in boot camps, online programs, community colleges, and industry, and had data science experts as key authors.

Among their findings and recommendations, which are best reviewed fully in their original report were:

- Data science is indeed appearing in numerous professional roles that extend from data analyst roles, and those who do work with data in organizations will likely need to gain more nuanced understandings as new techniques emerge and are taken up by different sectors
- Different sectors and roles will require different emphases, and this not only allows for university programs to customize for their populations and missions but also invites opportunities to generate more pathways for participation in data science regardless of where students start from
- This is becoming important enough that while specialized programs and integrations into specific existing departments (such as data science in biology or data science in finance), undergraduate institutions should be focusing on some data science exposure for all undergraduates
- Ethics and ethical practice need to be areas of emphasis not only for undergraduate institutions, courses, and programs but also for professional societies and groups to appropriately equip learners to practice data science responsibly
- This push for data science in undergraduate education is new enough that there should be active knowledge sharing across entities and institutions

Importantly, a specific goal of data science education should be the development of "data acumen" which will involve foundational knowledge that is typically from mathematics, computing, and statistics fields as well as covering data management and curation, data description, visualization, modeling, and assessment. Specific domains and fields would have their own considerations (e.g., how data work and techniques in social sciences may differ from physical sciences and within specific areas), but even with those differences, data acumen would include the ability to demonstrate communication, teamwork, workflow creation and participation, reproducability, and ethical problem solving with data.

Another document from NASEM was proceedings from a workshop held in 2022 in which panels and attendees were invited to meet and discuss key topics and questions related to K-12 data science education as an emerging field. The report document from that workshop (NASEM, 2023), which summarizes many of the conversations and also includes pointers to commissioned papers and a number of recent K-12 data science education projects, identifies a number of key challenges to consider moving forward. This book and that report are intended to be complementary.

Currently, NASEM is completing a consensus study report, mentioned earlier, that has been informed by the two other NASEM reports mentioned above (from 2018 and 2023) that helps speak to new competences in a world filled with data, computing, and rapid technological change. Likely, new reports to further build on all of these will come whether they involve questions of implementation, equity, and integration into other disciplines, or assessment.

Beyond this, there are valuable documents separate from NASEM's to review to get more familiar with important topics in the growing field of data science education research. For statistics education, the *International Handbook of Statistics Education* (2017) is a useful resource for work that has been done primarily with undergraduates in mind but some work specifically for K-12. Ongoing conferences, meetings, and research journals such as the *International Conference on the Teaching of Statistics (ICOTS)* and the *Journal of Statistics and Data Science Education* are some visible examples. Journal special issues are increasing on this topic and are worth reviewing. The GAISE II report completed in 2020 was the product of much intensive review and thought from leading statistics educators and provides guidance.

Books that turn a lens on what is happening with the explosion of data science, and especially those that serve as important warnings for how things can go poorly, include *Weapons of Math Destruction* by Cathy O'Neil, *Algorithms of Oppression* (2018) by Safiya Noble, *Race after Technology* (2019) by Ruha Benjamin, *Data Feminism* (2020) by Catherine D'Ignazio and Lauren Klein. A recent research volume, *Equity in Data Science* (2024), edited by Colby Tofel-Grehl and Emmanuel Schanzer, is another valuable resource sharing recent work in education and education research around data science education. *How Data Happened* (2023) by Chris Wiggins and Matthew Jones is a nice recent overview of historical developments leading to our current societal interest in data science.

This listing is far from exhaustive and does not include the ongoing stream of publications, commissioned papers, white papers, academic journals, and resource sites that are valuable. This can be a good starter library, and should expand in service of individual interests and new developments.

Closing

Looking forward, there is clearly a lot of work to be done related to data science education for K-12 simply on the research and development side. Schools and educational systems, however, cannot wait until everything is "all figured out" before taking action. Many are not waiting that long and are key partners in pushing new models forward. This need for some action, even in the face of incomplete and changing research, is common for K-12 education as it marches onward and continuously serves young people. Research is not historically known to be a fast-moving process.

While itself a topic of future research, it does appear that more models of partnership between schools and research organizations will need to be developed and modeled. Real intentional support for professional development and educator preparation, including the provision of time, materials, and funding, will be essential. Unfortunately, this can be treated as an afterthought or not even mentioned when new standards or guidelines are issued.

There are likely to be debates and disagreements about what roles everyone should play—data scientists, industry, government, parents, academics, teachers, toolmakers, and nonprofits among those. There may be complicated discussions about how to structure the school experience or curriculum to allow for a K-12 data science education approach that can make a meaningful impact on students. However, research can be an important input on this journey, and the information from this book should be one starting guide for those who are looking to embark on it.

Note

1 In full disclosure, I am one of the members of that committee, although the charge for the committee was written before my selection to be on it.

References

Agesilaou, A., & Kyza, E. A. (2022). Whose data are they? Elementary school students' conceptualization of data ownership and privacy of personal digital data. *International Journal of Child-Computer Interaction, 33*, 100462. https://doi.org/10.1016/j.ijcci.2022.100462

Ames, M. G. (2019). *The charisma machine: The life, death, and legacy of One Laptop per Child*. Cambridge: MIT Press.

Anderson, J. R., Corbett, A. T., Koedinger, K. R., & Pelletier, R. (1995). Cognitive tutors: Lessons learned. *Journal of the Learning Sciences, 4*(2), 167–207. https://doi.org/10.1207/s15327809jls0402_2

Austin, K., Ehrlich, S. B., Puckett, C., & Singleton, J. (2011). *YOUmedia Chicago reimagining learning, literacies, and libraries: A snapshot of year 1*, Chicago, IL. Retrieved from https://consortium.uchicago.edu/sites/default/files/2018-10/6899youmedia_final_2011.pdf

Benjamin, R. (2019). *Race after technology: Abolitionist tools for the new jim code*. New York: Polity Books.

Ben-Zvi, D., Makar, K., & Garfield, J. (Eds.). (2017). *International handbook of research in statistics education*. Cham: Springer.

Blikstein, P. (2018). Maker Movement in Education: History and Prospects. In M. J. de Vries (Ed.), *Handbook of Technology Education* (pp. 419–437). Cham: Springer International Publishing.

Bowler, L., Acker, A., Jeng, W., & Chi, Y. (2017). "It lives all around us": Aspects of data literacy in teen's lives. *Proceedings of the Association for Information Science and Technology, 54*(1), 27–35. https://doi.org/10.1002/pra2.2017.14505401004

Cognition & Technology Group at Vanderbilt. (1990). Anchored instruction and its relationship to situated cognition. *Educational Researcher, 19*(6), 2–10.

Cuban, L. (2001). *Oversold and underused: Computers in the classroom*. Cambridge, MA: Harvard University Press.

D'Ignazio, C., & Klein, L. F. (2020). *Data feminism*. Cambridge: MIT Press.

diSessa, A. A. (2000). *Changing minds: Computers, learning, and literacy*. Cambridge: MIT Press.

Gomez, L. M., Fishman, J. B., & Pea, D. R. (1998). The CoVis project: Building a large-scale science education testbed*. *Interactive Learning Environments, 6*(1–2), 59–92. https://doi.org/10.1076/ilee.6.1.59.3608

Gould, R., Machado, S., Johnson, T. A., & Molynoux, J. (2018). *Introduction to data science v 5.0*. Los Angeles, CA: UCLA Center X.

Jiang, S., Lee, V. R., & Rosenberg, J. M. (2022). Data science education across the disciplines: Underexamined opportunities for K-12 innovation. *British Journal of Educational Technology, 53*(2), 1073–1079. https://doi.org/10.1111/bjet.13258

Levitt, S. (2019). America's math curriculum doesn't add up. *Freakonomics* [Audio Podcast]: Freakonomics.

Linn, M. C., & Hsi, S. (2000). *Computers, teachers, peers: Science learning partners*. Mahwah, NJ: Lawrence Erlbaum Associates.

National Academies of Sciences, Engineering, and Medicine. (2018). *Data science for undergraduates: Opportunities and options*. Washington, DC: National Academies Press.

National Academies of Sciences, Engineering, and Medicine. (2023). *Foundations of data science for students in grades K-12: Proceedings of a workshop*. Washington, DC: The National Academies Press.

National Council of Teachers of Mathematics. (2024). *Teaching data science in high school: Enhancing opportunities and success*. Retrieved from https://www.nctm.org/Standards-and-Positions/Position-Statements/Teaching-Data-Science-in-High-School_-Enhancing-Opportunities-and-Success/

Noble, S. U. (2018). *Algorithms of oppression: How search engines reinforce racism*. New York, NY: New York University Press.

O'Neil, C. (2016). *Weapons of math destruction: How big data increases inequality and threatens democracy*. New York, NY: Broadway Books.

Papert, S. (1980). *Mindstorms: Children, computers, and powerful ideas*. New York, NY: Basic Books.

Pea, R., & Linn, M. C. (2020). Personal perspectives on the emergence of the learning sciences: 1970s–2005. *Frontiers in Education, 5*. https://doi.org/10.3389/feduc.2020.00130

Roschelle, J., & Pea, R. D. (2002). A walk on the WILD side: How wireless handhelds may change computer-supported collaborative learning. *International Journal of Cognition and Technology, 1*(1), 145–168.

Scardamalia, M., & Bereiter, C. (2006). Knowledge building: Theory, pedagogy, and technology. In K. Sawyer (Ed.), *Cambridge Handbook of the Learning Sciences* (pp. 97–118). New York, NY: Cambridge University Press.

Soloway, E., Norris, C., Blumenfeld, P., Fishman, B. J., Krajcik, J., & Marx, R. W. (2001). Palm-computing devices are ready-at-hand. *Communications of the ACM, 44*(6), 15–20.

Tofel-Grehl, C., & Schanzer, E. (2024). *Improving equity in data science: Re-imagining the teaching and learning of data in K-16 Classrooms.* New York: Taylor & Francis.

Wiggins, C., & Jones, M. L. (2023). *How data happened: A history from the age of reason to the age of algorithms.* New York: WW Norton & Company.

Wing, J. M. (2006). Computational thinking. *Communications of the ACM, 49*(3), 33–35.

Index

Note: **Bold** page numbers refer to tables; *italic* page numbers refer to figures and page numbers followed by "n" denote endnotes.

accessibility 98
accessible 28, 65, 85, 125, 144
activity trackers 60, 90, 110
Advanced Placement 28, 124
aggregate **25,** 39, 63–65, 67, 69, 115, 145
algebra: 2(as in Algebra 2) 30, 39, 82; advanced 33; linear **24,** 47
algorithm 7, 14, 34, 36, 38–39, 67, 72, 83, 117, 122; of oppression 147
Amazon Web Services 41, 43, 140
artificial intelligence 8–11, 15n2, 39, 51, 73, 84, 124, 140; and ChatGPT 7–10, 37
athletes 111–113, 126; and Esports 114; and students 112

Ben-Zvi, D. 64, 69, 115
big data 4, 60, 128–129, 133
bioinformatics 97, 140
Boaler, J. 2, 33, 72, 83, 142
Board of Admissions and Relations with Schools (BOARS) 30
Bureau of Labor Statistics 5–6, 40, 62

calculus 33, 39–40
California Mathematics Framework 2, 32–33, 82
cards 79, 80, 83, 91
case value 62, 64, 67
census **27,** 86, 105, 107

central tendency 63
citizen science 116
classifier **28,** 63
cleaning data 7, 41, 45
clustering **24,** 29, 39, 43, 63–64, 82
CODAP 84, 86, 93, 94, 96, 142
co-design 84
cognitive psychology 13, 19, 52, 83, 143
Common Core 38
community data 116
computational thinking 38, 72, 108, 139
computer science 3, 9, 20, 22, 82, 88, 108, 138–139, 141
Concord Consortium 142
Conway, D. 19, *20,* 21, 24–25, 34
copyright 8, 138
correlation 54, 70–71, 82
cosine similarity 18, 34, 39, 94
COVID-19 117, 128
critical 4–5, 14, 83, 90, 96, 117, 122–123, 128, 130, 134

database 7, **24,** 26, 40–41, 91, 94
data cycle 29, 36, *37,* 81, *82,* 87
Data Feminism 130–133
data moves 44, 91
data-science-as-content 34–35, 38–41, 44, 47
data-science-as-process 34–35, 37–40, 45, 81
Data Science 4 Everyone 142

data scientist 3, 6–7, 21–22, 31, 33–35, 37, 39, 40, 43–46, 62, 94, 108, 123, 131, 148
data structures 59, 88
datum 1, 62–63, 67, 128
decision tree **24,** 29, 82–83, 114
density 39, 56–57, 65, 67, 105
diabetes 115, 127
distribution 14, **28,** 38, 45, 63–64, 66–70, 81, 91, 107, 142, 145

employment 7, 86
ethics 20, 28, 29, 73, 90, 146
Excel 37, 42, 45, 94
exploratory data analysis **22,** 56, 79
exponent 30, 39, 83

financial literacy 31, 141
Freakonomics 141–142

GAISE 35, 67, 147; II 35–36, 45, 81
GDPR 133
GitHub 39, 42
Google 23, 41, 46, 47, 94, 108

histograms **27,** 28–29, 46, 56, 63, 82, 88
humanistic 125–126

indigenous 86, 133–134
inequalities 30, 40, 132
infographics 57, 85–86, 116
informal inference 69
integrated 14, 83
Introduction to Data Science 28, 36, 81, 142

Jupyter Notebooks 39, 41, 83, 94

Kaggle 41–42, 108
Kahneman, D. 52–54, 72
Konold, C. 60–64, 67, 91
Kuhn, D. 55, 71

Lehrer, R. 66, 88
libraries 59, 105, 107–108, 139; of software 39, 45
local 65, 69, 81, 115–116
logarithmic 39, 83

machine learning 7–8, 24–26, 28–29, 39–41, 44, 47, 73, 87, 141
maker 87; movement 139; space 88, 140

map 57, 105, 129; cholera 62; MapReduce **24**
matrix 40, 59
mobile device 59, 110, 139, 144
model **23, 25, 27,** 28, 42–43, 84, 91, 94, 104, 109, 116–117, 130, 148; data modeling 88; as examples 1; of instruction 148; multi-level **25,** 26, 83
museum 105–107

National Academies of Science, Engineering, and Medicine 27, 29, 140, 145–147
National Science Foundation 11, 12, 15, 79, 104, 139
New York Times 1, 85–86, 94, 117
Noble, S. 132, 134, 147

objectivity 122, 132

phonics 30–31
photograph 89, 129–130
polynomial 30, 39
PPDAC 36
privacy 20, **28,** 59–60, 73, 90, 110, 115, 118, 133, 144
productivity 5, 9, 94, 110, 139
programming 22–23, 26, 28–29, 46, 72, 78, 81–83, 95, 126, 138–139, 143; language 23, 26, 29, 37–39, 41, 73, 94; toys 78
Python 23, **24,** 26, 29, 37, 40–42, 94

R 22–23, **25,** 26, 29, 37, 82, 94
regression **24, 28,** 29
RStudio 22, **25,** 26, 41, 94
Rubin, A. 69, 79, 106

sample 8, **28,** 35, 54, 59, 68–70, 79, 92; sampling **27,** 29, 67, 69–70, 82, 90
scatterplot 29, 46, 82, 85
sensor 37, 58, 87, 109, 112, 125–126
simulation 42, 70, 72, 93
social studies 14, 85–87, 137
SQL **24,** 41–42
standalone 14
statisticians 6–7, 25, 35–36
story 8, 35, 89, 93, 111, 117, 124, 130, 139; telling 42, 45, 89, 93
subjective 115, 126–128
survey 37, 41, 42, 62

TERC 79, 81, 106
tidy 22, 23, 41, 128
TinkerPlots 91–92, *131*

undergraduate 5, 27, 57, 68, 108, 123, 145–146

variability 34, 38, 61, 64, 66–67, 81; measurement 67; natural 66–67; sampling 67, 70
variables 4, 22, 36, 43, 65–67, 70–71, 87–88

Venn diagram 19–21, 24, 34
video 4, 9, 110, 117, 123, 129–130; gaming 114
visualization 9, 11, 14, 22–23, 40, 43–47, 62, 68, 78, 80, 84–86, 88, 94, 95, 98, 105, 107–108, 111, 138, 146; common types 29, 33–34, 40, 46; difficulties with 56–59; novel 89, 117; tools 80, 91–95

Wilkerson, M. 12, 93, 125